Young People, Bereavement and Loss

Disruptive transitions?

Available in alternative formats

This publication can be provided in alternative formats, such as large print, Braille, audiotape and on disk. Please contact: Communications Department, Joseph Rowntree Foundation, The Homestead, 40 Water End, York YO30 6WP. Tel: 01904 615905. Email: info@jrf.org.uk

Young People, Bereavement and Loss

Disruptive transitions?

Jane Ribbens McCarthy with Julie Jessop

JOSEPH ROWNTREE
FOUNDATION

national
children's
bureau

Joseph Rowntree Foundation

The Joseph Rowntree Foundation has supported this project as part of its programme of research and innovative development projects, which it hopes will be of value to policy-makers, practitioners and service users.

National Children's Bureau

NCB promotes the voices, interests and well-being of all children and young people across every aspect of their lives. As an umbrella body for the children's sector in England and Northern Ireland, we provide essential information on policy, research and best practice for our members and other partners.

NCB aims to:

- challenge disadvantage in childhood
- work with children and young people to ensure they are involved in all matters that affect their lives
- promote multidisciplinary cross-agency partnership and good practice
- influence government through policy development and advocacy
- undertake high quality research and work from an evidence-based perspective
- disseminate information to all those working with children and young people, and to children and young people themselves.

The views expressed in this book are those of the authors and not necessarily those of the National Children's Bureau, the Joseph Rowntree Foundation or the Open University.

Published by the National Children's Bureau for the Joseph Rowntree Foundation

National Children's Bureau, 8 Wakley Street, London EC1V 7QE
Tel: 020 7843 6000
Website: www.ncb.org.uk
Registered Charity number 258825

Published 2005

ISBN 1 904 787 45 2

British Library Cataloguing in Publication Data
A catalogue record for this book is available from the British Library

Contents

Acknowledgements

The various members of the project team over time, which has included Julie Jessop, Wendy Martin and Sue Sharpe, as well as Jane Ribbens McCarthy, and our editor, Lynn Eaton, along with invaluable input from the library staff at the Open University, particularly Kelvin Street.

Individuals and organisations who have been generous with their thoughts and time as we have developed the draft report.

Those enormously helpful people who have commented on the lengthy original draft manuscript (although we are responsible for any deficiencies in the content of the final production). They are: Dr Graham Crow (University of Southampton); Professor Jenny Hockey (University of Sheffield); Dr Carol Ann Hooper (University of York); Wendy Martin (University of Warwick); Barbara Monroe (Chief Executive, St Christopher's Hospice, London); Liz Rolls (University of Sheffield); Professor Helen Sweeting (University of Glasgow).

Our project managers, Charlie Lloyd at the Joseph Rowntree Foundation (who has been very patient indeed with various setbacks), and Professors John Muncie and Janet Newman at the Open University (who have been both patient and practically supportive), as well as other colleagues at the OU who have had to live with my continual preoccupation with bereavement and young people.

Professor Janet Holland (South Bank University) and Rachel Thomson (Open University) for generously allowing us to develop the case studies from data sets held at South Bank University.

The Joseph Rowntree Foundation for funding the project and allowing us the time to complete it.

Prologue: Tragedy

Tragedy, no one could prepare you, words seem muffled, your chest splits open, the heart skips a million beats then falls slowly but surely to the ground. You try to grab it but it's gone, you're hollow, empty.

You're joking ... A classic line that's said when faced with such news and of course they're not.

The feeling is like some one pushing hard on your chest, there's air in there but you can't breathe, it's trapped like your state of mind, you're in a thousand places at one time and there's no way out, not now.

So you're on the floor, tears streaming, they roll gently down your cheek until you can taste the salt in the crease of your mouth. It was a grazed knee the last time you tasted it, so much sweeter then.

You're lifted, you're standing, you're stitched up and beating again, then suddenly it all becomes too much and you're back where you started only ten times worse.

Back straight, head hung low, eyes wide and puffy, nose running and lips quivering. You find yourself staring at a plant, it's ugly but you look at it anyway, both hands held, both legs crossed all eyes on you.

You're in shock now: there's no realisation, it can't be true, how could it, things like this don't happen to me, I hear you say. But every so often you get a sudden rush of fear, it encloses you with all its power. That's the feeling you get when you believe that this could actually be happening – which it is.

Two months, six months, it still comes, that feeling and that tear rolling. Certain things, a smell, a song, a memory, but you grab your heart this time and stick it back in your chest.

No one can prepare you for a tragedy.

Rebecca Wills

(Age 15 - six months after the death of her step-father)

Introduction

Bereavement and young people

Death is never an easy topic to contemplate, raising questions about our own mortality, the meaning of life, and profound issues of human relationships. And in the context of thinking about youth, it may be viewed as a major anomaly, a particularly unwelcome and untimely subject (the association of death with ageing is, however, quite recent in origin). But, while bereavement is often regarded as a source of disruption, youth too may be seen as disruptive in its own right. The conjunction of the two, then, might be understood as a 'double jeopardy'.

This report is concerned with bereavement and its implications for the lives of young people in contemporary western societies, particularly in the UK. While there has been extensive research in recent decades focusing on the implications of disruption through divorce and separation, disruption due to bereavement has not received the same attention. And yet the questions raised in the existing literature are important ones: from the possible implications of parental death for long-term risk of depression, to the frequency of experiences of bereavement among young offenders; from the desirability of including death and bereavement as a general feature of the school curriculum, to how best to make help available to bereaved young people who have no-one to talk to.

The neglect of the topic may have occurred because society feels it is too uncomfortable to contemplate. But a key argument of this report is that the issue requires more direct attention from mainstream policies and services for young people. At the same time, we argue that bereavement may not always be experienced as an unmitigated loss: rather, it is a source of change, and change always has the potential for gains as well as losses, even where it may be – sometimes unbearably – hard to live through. 'Loss' as a concept, however, has a long, varied and distinguished theoretical history (for example, Bowlby, Freud). We discuss these terms, and the definitions of bereavement, grief and mourning, at much greater length in the related book publication (Ribbens McCarthy, 2006, forthcoming).

This project set out to review the relevant literature, with possible lines of question being:

1. What do we know about young people's experiences of bereavement, in both the shorter and longer term?
2. What do we know about the sorts of 'outcomes' that may be associated, in terms of behavioural correlates?
3. What do we know about agencies' awareness of, and responsiveness to, such issues?
4. What are the underlying theoretical assumptions underpinning current knowledge?
5. What methodologies have been used to study these issues, and how do they link to particular theoretical frameworks?

It may be immediately apparent, however, that 'bereavement' may cover a great variety of experiences and relationships. Some bereavements may be experienced as particularly 'significant'. Others may be experienced as less disruptive but, nevertheless, raise significant issues about relationships and the meaning of mortality.

Any form of relationship that is disrupted by death may be experienced as a bereavement (and some authors would extend the concept to cover other sources of disruption in relationships). Much of the specialist literature that we consider in this report is centred on 'family' relationships, particularly the death of a parent during childhood and youth, while the death of a sibling has also received attention in recent years. Bereavement due to the death of a peer has received only marginal attention from both the research literature and the organisation of specialist services, and yet this may be experienced as a highly 'significant' bereavement in its own right.

Other forms of bereavement are hardly mentioned in the context of youth, whether by miscarriage or abortion, the death of a baby or child, the death of a partner, or of a pet. And yet, whether or not a particular bereavement is felt to be significant in the life of a young person cannot be 'read off' from the category of the relationship, but depends on the meaning that relationship holds for the individual young person. This makes it a difficult topic to research and draw firm conclusions from.

At present, it is even difficult to find clear evidence about the frequency with which certain forms of bereavement are experienced by young people. What is very striking to us as researchers is that we cannot even answer, with any level of confidence, the apparently straightforward question of the numbers experiencing parental death. Nevertheless, a broad picture can be tentatively pieced together.

How common is bereavement among young people?

We might assume that the major historical decline in early mortality (Anderson 1985, 1990), and the absence of wars involving large numbers of young people from western countries over the last 60 years, will mean that children and young people are unlikely to experience bereavement, but this is not so. While the existing evidence is not clear about the frequency of experience of particular categories of death (see Appendix), overall, the great majority (as high as 92 per cent) of young people in the UK do report having experienced bereavement with regard to what they consider to be a 'close' or 'significant' relationship (sometimes including pets), before the age of 16 (Harrison and Harrington 2001). Such experiences will be even more common by the age of 18 or 25.

While many of these bereavements concern the death of a grandparent, the death of a parent before age 16 is not as uncommon as might be supposed. Figures range from 3.9 per cent (Sweeting and others 1998) to 7.4 per cent (Wadsworth 1991). Figures for the death of a sibling are harder to establish, but seem to be similar to (or perhaps slightly lower than) figures for death of a parent (Harrison and Harrington 2001). The majority of sibling deaths will concern the death of an infant.

The prevalence of bereavement due to death of a close friend is yet more elusive to establish, but there is some evidence to suggest that this may be more common than these 'family' deaths. Meltzer and others (2000) found twice as many five- to 15-year-olds reported the death of a close friend as the death of a parent or sibling. The complexities and robustness of these various statistical sources are discussed further in the Appendix.

How is the prevalence of bereavement shaped by social circumstances?

We know that life expectancy varies very significantly by social class, geography and locality, and such health inequalities have widened in the UK in recent years (Shaw and others 1999). The risk of premature death (that is, before the age of 65) is almost three times greater in some parliamentary constituencies than others, and the risk of death is further related to living in deprived localities. So we would expect the experience of bereavement due to the death of a parent to vary significantly by social class and locality, with young people living in deprived areas being more likely to experience such a bereavement. The death of a sibling is likely to vary in similar ways: 'In Britain as a whole over one quarter of childhood deaths ... were attributable to social inequality' (Shaw and others 1999: 162).

This then raises further questions about what such variations in bereavement by social class and locality may mean for the social contexts, support and individual experience of bereavement. This is not a question that has been directly addressed by the existing literature, but it is one to which we return towards the end of this report.

The significance of social, historical and cultural contexts

Besides such variations between different sectors within the current UK context, experiences of bereavement may vary across contemporary societies (even between industrialised countries). Suicide rates among young people may vary between European countries (Beratis 1991), while violent deaths may be more common among young people in the USA (Balk 1995, and see Appendix). The relative significance of household disruption and (re)formation due to death or divorce may also vary across European countries (Iacovou and Berthoud 2001).

Along with such demographic variations across societies and across time (Anderson 1985, 1990), there have been major cultural shifts in the meaning of death, the social contexts of mourning and experiences of bereavement. It is highly debatable how we understand the subjective feelings of bereavement, and associated cultural practices, of those living in harsher circumstances than our own, whether we are looking across history (Strange 2002) or across societies (Eisenbruch 1991; Scheper-Hughes 1992; Scheper-Hughes and Sargent 1998). But many historians, sociologists and anthropologists (for example, Aries 1974, 1981; Elias 1985; Field 1996; Hockey 1990, 1996; Shilling 1993; Walter 1991, 1999) have argued that the historical trend towards secularisation, accompanied by the increasing medicalisation of death, has led to the 'sequestration of experience' (Giddens 1990, 1991), resulting in a public absence/private presence of death (Mellor 1993). Contemporary western societies, it is argued, have forgotten how to grieve (Gorer 1987; Small and Hockey 2001).

In our comparatively safe, secular, society, then, what support systems are there for bereaved young people? If religion does not play a big part in their life, where does a young person turn to help make sense of such difficult events? By contrast, if a young person lives in a society where violence and early death are pervasive and highly visible, direct personal experience of death, and a contemplation of one's own death, may be commonplace (Amaya 2002).

The importance of cultural differences and associated rituals of mourning, and how they affect bereavement in contemporary multicultural Britain, has received increasing attention from those working professionally in this field (Green 1991, Neuberger 1987; Parkes and others 1997). There can be a danger, however, of cultural stereotyping, and some authors suggest that 'cultural sensitivity' alone is not enough when dealing with bereavement (Desai and Bevan 2002). In this report, we have not looked explicitly at how different cultures in the UK deal with bereavement, but have taken a more inclusive approach.

This report

The literature review on which we embarked turned out to be more extensive and challenging than originally anticipated, and the research evidence to be fraught with contradictions. This report is an edited version of our findings and discussion, full details of which are due to be published as a book by Open University Press (Ribbens McCarthy 2006, forthcoming). The book will develop the arguments here and present more detailed discussion of the research evidence and the assumptions on which it is based. It will particularly consider the significance of taking an interdisciplinary and pluralist methodological approach towards this important substantive issue, arguing for a respect and dialogue across disciplinary, and academic and professional, boundaries. In this regard, bereavement in the lives of young people constitutes a significant topic that may encourage us all to re-examine our assumptions and approaches to dealing with such disruptions, in the context of the practical, social and spiritual challenges of major life change.

We start this report by presenting case studies of individual young people, along with other evidence of how young people themselves discuss their experiences of bereavement (Chapter 1). In Chapter 2 we consider the different ways in which the topic may be theorised and researched, and the approach taken in our literature review. We then turn in Chapter 3 to an examination of the empirical evidence of bereavement as a 'risk factor' in the individual lives of young people. Chapter 4 considers the social contexts of bereavement, and approaches to education and intervention. In the concluding chapter we seek to pull together the implications for policy makers and practitioners who are trying to develop best procedures and practice.

We hope that both the book and this report will help those involved with working with young people – across the broad range of mainstream as well as specialist services – to respond imaginatively and rigorously to this issue in young people's lives.

1. Young people's experiences of bereavement

By Sue Sharpe, Jane Ribbens McCarthy and Julie Jessop

Introduction

Insights into young people's own perspectives on experiences of bereavement can be gained from a range of materials and sources, which we consider in this chapter. We start by introducing three young people who were interviewed over some years, not as part of a research project on bereavement issues, but as participants in a general longitudinal study of the lives of young people. In the course of the repeated interviews, these young people happened to talk about experiences of bereavement, and so we got a rare chance to gain some in-depth insights, over time, about how such issues may be experienced by 'ordinary' young people who are just getting on with their lives.

Not all these bereavements were experienced as major disruptions, but they were all important life events that were discussed at some length in the interviews, and this *range* of experiences points to the variations in the meaning of bereavement for young people more generally, that need to be considered and included in terms of their policy and professional implications.

Following these case studies, we turn to consider other available qualitative evidence about how young people may experience bereavement in their lives. Much of this latter evidence – as with much of the research evidence considered in subsequent chapters – is clearly focused on bereavements that have constituted highly disruptive life events that young people themselves may feel have 'set them apart'. In this sense, they represent a particular element of the range of possible experiences of bereavement.

Box 1.1: Background to the case studies

The case studies are derived from work undertaken by a team of researchers at South Bank University (headed by Professor Janet Holland and Rachel Thomson),[1] with young people in five different research locations, some of whom have been followed up in successive studies over a period of six years. In analysing the interviews, the researchers identified those young people who talked about bereavement or death in the course of narrating their lives overall. From these, we then selected three case studies to represent a range of experiences and situations, but all from young people who had not been identified as 'problematic' by any form of statutory body, and had not received any particular interventions in connection with their bereavements. We were thus able to gain some insight into how 'ordinary' young people may deal with bereavement in the absence of any such interventions.

The interviews were analysed by Sue Sharpe,[2] who had not been involved in other aspects of the current literature review, and therefore had no particular knowledge of existing evidence about bereavement and young people. She was given the brief to immerse herself in the individual accounts, to consider the major themes and events the young people themselves narrated in their interviews.[3]

Notes

1. We are indebted to South Bank University for providing access to these materials. Further details of the studies and associated publications can be found at www.sbu.ac.uk/fhss/ff/. The three studies were funded by the Economic and Social Research Council in its programmes on Childhood (6–16), and Youth, and within the Family and Social Capital ESRC Research Group, respectively.

2. Sue Sharpe was one of the researchers working on a consultancy basis on the original studies. The other core members of the research team were Sheila Handerson, Janet Holland, Sheena McGrellis and Rachel Thomson; Robert Bell, Rebecca Taylor and Tina Grigorio have also been involved with different stages of the project.

3. The related book (Ribbens McCarthy 2006, forthcoming) gives the full narratives from the three case studies, along with a further two case studies. We have here, for the sake of brevity, included only the interviewees' comments on bereavement. In doing so, we have obviously had to lose the sense of narrative element and much of the context of the overall life history which would otherwise form the core of this kind of research.

Shirleen

Shirleen was first interviewed at school, aged 13, and has been interviewed five times since then, most recently at age 18, by which time she had moved on to college. She lives with her mother in a two-bedroom flat in a large city. Her mother and father were both originally from Jamaica, and have family both here and back in the West Indies. Her parents were divorced before Shirleen's first interview.

For Shirleen, her family – and she has a large one – has always played a very important part in her life. It was when she was about 12 or 13 that a family illness and death – her great-grandfather in Jamaica – had made her think more about herself and life in general:

> ... some things that happen, like small things, have made me like who I am, but they haven't been like serious major things, I think I've been more, well my great-grandfather died, it was about a couple of years ago and even though, like I knew he was ill ... I went to Jamaica so I could get to know him more, but when he died I think it made me realise that I can't waste the time and seeing that the years are going by so quickly, I don't really have time, I feel like they're just slipping from underneath me sometimes, like a day will come and then the next day is gone ... 'cause of that it made me realise that I don't have much time to waste.

She described how this bereavement had led her to become even more of a 'family person':

> ... since then I've like stayed around my family a bit more, more of a family person ... since he did die, had more of a family connection and with my grandad as well, because he reminds me of him, 'cause my grandad's kind of ill. My grandad's over here, it's not that far so I go down and see my Nan and grandad every week ... I just like to spend time with my grandparents more, since my great-grandad died, 'cause I feel like, because they're older, like my grandad's quite ill and so is my Nan as well, so I spend more time with them 'cause like sometime they could be gone so I try and spend as much time with them as I can.

It was her great-grandfather's death, together with her mother's strict encouragement, that helped to make Shirleen realise years later that she needed to get on and do things with her life. But at this stage, she was also beginning to realise that there was in fact some time to do things:

> I feel like I've still got a lot to learn and there's still a lot of things that I don't know that I wanna know, that's what my mum says sometimes, I'm a bit too eager [laughs] and to learn everything as soon as possible but now I know that I've got more time than like I thought I had so I can just really kick back for a couple of years and you know, I still got all my life to grow up and do what I wanna do.

Commentary

The death of her great-grandfather in Jamaica was discussed at various points in these interviews over the years. We can therefore understand the significance of this death in terms of Shirleen's quest to understand her family history and its links with Jamaica, and thus a key feature of her identity as a black person in a situation of migration and diaspora.

Shirleen's understanding of the meaning of the death changed over time. She expressed rather contradictory views in her last interview, about how far she still thought life needs to be lived in a hurry. But the bereavement continued to represent an important element in the way in which she understood her life, leading her to ponder life's brevity and significance, and to want to make her life purposeful.

Neville

Neville was interviewed five times between the ages of 17 and 22. He comes from a Protestant family living in a city in Northern Ireland. At the time of the first full interview, aged 18, Neville was very keen on cars. He had finally taken and passed his driving test not long before Christmas – but soon after he crashed the family car.

A couple of weeks later he was in the house with his mother when she collapsed. He had tried to resuscitate her but it did not work and she died. It was something to do with her heart and totally unexpected because she had been very healthy, never ill, and there were no signs of anything wrong. It was a very traumatic thing to deal with:

> I don't think I ever will [get over it] because the picture that's stuck clear in my head, you know, what happened that day ... I can remember as if it was yesterday you know. It's that strong and it's five months ago nearly. I just have to go on you know, the family just decided to go on you know and not to dwell on the past and to go on. And that was it.

Family life was at a standstill as Neville, his father and older sister, tried to take in what had happened: 'We were just walking around like zombies you know. We weren't functioning as a team anymore'.

Neville's father had taken two weeks off work. He was reading a book on 'bereavement' and decided that the first thing was to get back into some routine:

> So we decided to just get ourselves together and just sorta play through things like you know, doing the ironing once or twice a week or whatever ...

> just a routine ... to try get some sort of thing going. Because if you don't like, you'll just fall apart and you're finished.

His father also decided that the best thing for them all was to return to work or college. Neville found the first week back at the Tech very hard:

> When I went in the first day and sat through two hours of class and went out to lunch then for about an hour and went up and bought a leather jacket, the one you see sitting on the chair, and came back and said I can't do this. I went home then and came back the next day and then I started then back. But it was the first day back after she died that was the hardest. And then after that I kind of was back to full steam then.

He talked of how he was determined to work hard, and to keep doing well and get another distinction at college for the sake of his mother.

Neville's friends were supportive when his mother died. They rang up and called round and were generally supportive. He did not always want to be sociable, but he really appreciated their efforts:

> I noticed that when my mum died they all came round to the house and it was great you know ... they just dropped whatever they were doing to come here ... I mean, I don't know how many offers I had to go out and everything would be paid for but I just didn't feel like it at that stage you know ... they helped me through it and they know it too because I told them that many times. And they said it's not because we took pity on you it was because you are a friend.

Just over a year after his mother's death, Neville, aged 19, was still doing well in college, he had a good relationship with his father, his sister was engaged and life had settled down. He had had a girlfriend for a few months and really enjoyed being in a steady relationship, but she suddenly cooled off and they split up.

He found constant reminders of his mother:

> It's um ... easing up a wee bit. Och, it's hard but you just have to go on and stuff and you know, it's easy to say that but ... it's ... just have good days and bad days and things. Maybe something will trigger me off like photographs. We've a pile of photographs in the house and um ... I just can't get over it at times ... when it's really hard, it's like losing part of yourself and then you know that part of yourself, and you just have to ... it's like learning to walk again ...

> I'm finding it a bit harder. Maybe the rest of them are just coping with it or looking as if they're coping with it but I'm not. There's times when I really don't cope at all. You know, I'm in this house nearly every night and maybe I've been working on an assignment and then you know, something just reminds me of my mum or you know, you walk past that hall ...

There were also times when he wished he could get away from everything:

> There's times like I just feel like saying 'Oh to hell with it all' and you know, going away somewhere and just starting again ... there is times like I don't want to go out or I don't want to do this or I don't want to do that ... It's just very hard to explain like. Okay, a year's gone past now like and it's still as bad ... It still hurts like hell and you know, there's nothing you can do. You can't bring her back. You can't change time or anything but it's just a struggle at times and other times, I can cope for a couple of weeks and not really think about her. But you know, the next day I'll be thinking about her non stop just and it goes through my head all of this, you know, what happened, what – what I did, and what could've have happened, and all this crap and I just can't do anything really about it like and ...

As Neville recounted in the third interview, at age 20, his mother's death still loomed large for him and he sometimes drove up to the graveyard, parked in the car park and talked to her:

> I would go late at night (to the graveyard) but I wouldn't actually go down. There's like a wee car park thing and ... I would just sit there and talk. Just to ... you know ... it's only a grave, talk into the grave but I wouldn't actually go down to the grave. I would just sit in the car – for 10 minutes or whatever and just talk and I would come out then a bit refreshed.

At this point in time, he felt that his mother's death had changed him:

> It's changed me as a person. I do think that. You know, I'm not as out-going as I was before ... I think I'm a more emotional person now ... I'd be crying a lot more now. Well, I wouldn't be crying at everything ... but I wouldn't be as strong as I was before. And I find it hard to get motivated most of the time now ... but if I really try now ... you know, I'll try and get something done because I want to pass this course.

To mark the second anniversary of his mother's death, he had written up the whole event in great detail:

> But what I did do this year is on the 8th January I sat down at the lap-top and wrote the whole thing out, from start to finish ... I just sat down and

> typed, I can even remember conversations we were having on that day and who came in and if somebody came in and what I said to them and blah, blah. It took me 10 pages to write it but it was so, just like somebody lifting a weight off your shoulders because I kept it in for two years and I just thought right, I was meaning to do it but I didn't know when to do it and I thought I'll do it on the anniversary two years on because it means more, do you know what I mean.

He had shown it to his sister but not his father yet, and had also left it with a tutor at college. But not for them to suggest any changes:

> ... I mean it's like I don't want to touch it, I don't want to reword what I wrote because on the day that's how I felt. There's no point me rewording it now but because it just wouldn't be the same. I felt better for doing it.

Although he and his father had established a way of life together, Neville was aware that it would be his 21st birthday in a few months, and he thought it would be rather different from his sister's a few years before:

> I was wondering around birthdays – just like I'll be 21 now in June and when my sister was 21 she got a big surprise party. That won't happen, well it might happen but not in the same way. So it will be a sad time.

Losing someone so close, and in such a sudden manner, has left him with underlying concerns for those nearest to him, his father and sister:

> I would be worried about it if he's not up before me in the morning ... or if I shout him and he's not answering me I would be worried about that because I'm worried that, you know, something could happen ... I would worry about Bridget, if somebody rang up and say Bridget's in hospital I would drop everything, it doesn't matter where I am, you know that type of thing.

When interviewed nearly two years later, aged 22, Neville had completed his HND course but decided not to pursue university even though he had been offered a place. He felt he had lost some of his previous confidence to do well. His sister had got married, an event that underlined the absence of his mother. He had let his friends go a bit during the last year or so, and was still seeking a steady relationship for himself.

Commentary

It seems that Neville continued for some years with his aims and ambitions, despite not really coming to terms with his mother's death, and did well at college.

His decision not to go on to university remains a puzzle, but perhaps it was linked to his expressed loss of confidence and motivation.

While his family and friends had been very important and helped to sustain him through these difficult years, the successive interviews also seemed to suggest that he had become more isolated as time went on. He regularly returned to the theme of the depth of devastation, and absence of opportunities to talk. The death itself, which was clearly a traumatic experience, also continued to preoccupy Neville over the years.

Brian

Brian, who comes from a working-class area in the north-west of England, was interviewed four times. He was still at school for the first two, aged 15 and 16, and at college for the latter two, aged 17 and 19 years. He has had some learning difficulties, and was sometimes bullied, although he went on to take GCSEs.

During the year before the first interview, his father had developed cancer in his lung, which although treated recurred six months later. After some weeks it moved to his brain and he died in the spring. Talking about this in the interview a couple of months after the funeral it was clear that this had shattered the earlier security of Brian's life. He had done his best to help his mother look after his father as he got increasingly frail, and now he was concerned about his mother and how he could help her to cope.

> My mum says just be your normal charming self and help us through it. My mum said she can never be sad when I'm around, 'cause I helped us through it and also helped my dad when he was very poorly, I had to lift him up, mum said that's a great help.

When his father died, Brian had taken a couple of weeks off school, and people were quite supportive when he returned. His girlfriend Lisa, in particular, had helped and they used to have long talks on the phone in the evenings.

In his first interview, Brian recalled the special things he had enjoyed sharing with his father, particularly the 'magical Christmases' when decorating the Christmas tree, and he anticipated this would be a hard loss to face when the next Christmas came along.

> I've got all sorts of memories of dad really. Done a lot of good things, made every single Christmas magical ... yeah and so did my mum ... It's gonna be hard though 'cause every year me and dad used to put the lights on the

> tree, every year, so this year it's just gonna be down to me and my brother, and my mum.

A year later, when interviewed at 16, he described how this had been:

> ... life's been going alright, been feeling a bit sad now and then ... but the hardest part was at Christmas, Christmas Day morning, Mum said once we got the meal over Christmas Day, it's alright, but it was in the morning like opening the presents, and I missed him putting the lights up on the tree ... it weren't the same ... my brother did the lights and I was just hanging stuff up.

At the time of the second interview, Brian was still at school and contemplating GCSE exams with his father in mind: 'Probably gonna get on [with the exams] okay, another thing, dad's looking over and dad would want me to do well. That's what I think anyway.'

Although there was a sense of continuity in his life through his home and his family, the loss of Lisa, his girlfriend, had made a dent in this, and his father's tragic death was still very present in his mind. 'Sit there and think and it just makes me feel sad. Sometimes you think about it when you're sad but sometimes you think about it when you're happy, 'cause you remember all the good memories with him.'

He missed him a lot, and commented: 'the person close to you would be your dad, your best friend.'

Another year on in his life was to see two more deaths – his grandmother and his father's best friend.

> A lot has happened, as you know, there's been a lot of marriages, like there's been two weddings, but there's been a lot of deaths really, like my dad's best mate, and my gran, she died last week, so it's been quite a rough year really.

At this point, aged 17, he spoke of himself as being 'unlucky' because there was so much death in his life. He was still replaying his father's death sometimes, and wondering what life would have been like if his father had still been around for him:

> Yeah, still replay it back in my mind, even now, nearly two years ago, wonder what would happen if ... it's like wouldn't have got the cancer, would he still have been here now, often think that, I think would he be here now, or ... and he probably would have been the same as what he was like when he was here.

He also discussed his worries about the future for his mother: 'Most concerned about my mum a lot ... it's my mum that hardly goes out, I get worried sometimes.'

Commentary

When Brian was younger he did not seem to the interviewer to have much of a grasp on reality, although he had certainly taken in the reality of his father's death. And he appeared to have no real sense of the long term, and still has little of this. If his father had been there, he suggests, life might have been different, in terms of support for both himself and his mother, and he would still have him as his 'best friend'.

As the years passed between the interviews, Brian's accounts shifted from positive accounts of a stable life, to more apprehensive narratives of a life in which risks had become more apparent. The death of his father was a major event in his life, and, although his life did not appear to have taken too much of a turn for the worse as a result, his distress and regret clearly went deep and continued over the years of the interviews.

Combined with other losses and deaths of important people around him, Brian would appear to be potentially at risk in terms of his own need for support in the years to come. Nevertheless, his own major concern was with the needs of his mother.

Hearing the voices of young people

We hope that our case studies convey, to some degree, the depths and complexities of the different 'realities' narrated by these young people around their experiences of bereavement. But before we consider what general conclusions can be drawn from these case studies, we turn next to examine other materials available to us, through which we can hear the 'voices' of young people themselves.

In general terms, there has been a growth of social research that seeks to hear such 'voices', often drawing on the 'new' sociology of childhood (for example James and others 1998; Mayall 2002; Morrow 1998; Woodhead and Montgomery 2003), and often outside the theoretical framework of child development used by more psychologically based studies. But in the context of bereavement issues, there is generally a dearth of academic research which looks specifically at the perceptions and understandings of teenagers and young people.

Insights into the perspectives of bereaved young people can, however, be gained from a range of sources, sometimes in a more anecdotal way.

Box 1.2: Qualitative evidence of young people's perspectives on bereavement

Qualitative evidence of young people's perspectives includes personal autobiographical and retrospective experiences (for example Abrams 1992; Elliott 1999; Krementz 1983; Perschy 1997), and case studies and quotes used in the context of more structured, psychological research and theoretical frameworks (such as Balk 2000; Doka 2000; Worden 1996). Literature and resources that are oriented towards advice and interventions often include a variety of quotes and case studies of individual young people (for example Bode 1993; Levete 1998; Wallbank 1998; Wilby 1995), and some research projects have interviewed young people about their views on interventions (for example Holland 2001). Videos featuring young people, and on-line interactive resources available through websites hosted by help organisations (discussed further in Chapter 4), also enable young people to discuss their experiences. But in considering any of this material, it is important to bear in mind issues of *whose* voices are being heard, and *how* these voices are interpreted.[1]

Note

1. We discuss the various types of qualitative studies – their methodologies, implications, strengths and potential pitfalls – in more detail in Ribbens McCarthy (2006, forthcoming).

In exploring these sources, we can distinguish several particularly apparent overarching themes. First, young people described feelings that were new and overwhelming – as we heard in Rebecca's poem in the Prologue. These feelings were often not acknowledged and they did not know how to talk about them. Second, many of these accounts focused on features of their social relationships and general social settings. It is apparent that bereaved children and young people take their cues from those closest to them, which will vary in different cultural contexts, while family members may seek to 'protect' each other by avoiding painful conversations. Furthermore, the initial bereavement may be followed by losses through the breakdown of other relationships. Third, issues of time are significant. While time may be helpful for some, for others, grief can re-emerge at significant points in later life, with previously unexpressed grief sometimes emerging years later.

Callers to ChildLine

A further set of insights may be gained through research into the nature of calls made to ChildLine (Cross 2002), the UK free and anonymous telephone helpline that is available for children and young people to access for themselves.

Some of the concerns raised in calls centring on bereavement echo themes raised in other places, as discussed earlier. But there are some particular points that are quite strikingly different, perhaps precisely because of ChildLine's unique position in being accessible directly to young people at a time of their choosing. For example, many children seemed to have needed someone to talk to about their strong emotions very shortly after the death had occurred, sometimes making very brief calls of only one or two minutes. Other callers spoke of their surprise and fear at their own feelings, expressing a sense of not knowing how to behave.

Nearly 10 per cent of the sample of all bereaved callers spoke of wanting to die: 'Dad died when I was three. I sometimes think about killing myself because I want to be with him in heaven' (Cross 2002: 10).

A particularly disturbing feature of some of the calls (5 per cent altogether) was the presence of associated problems of abuse and neglect. For example: 'Dad came to my bed this morning. He said it wouldn't hurt. Mum died and I miss her' (Cross 2002: 11). The use of alcohol by adults dealing with difficult emotions is a regular feature of these quotes: 'Mum beats my little brother. She won't listen to me. She didn't drink until my stepdad died' (Cross 2002: 11).

The phone calls were primarily centred on loss of parents and grandparents. It is noteworthy that maternal deaths were the single most frequent category of bereavement, even though we know that children and young people are statistically more likely to lose a father than a mother through death. Other forms of loss included siblings, friends (including partners and ex-partners), pets, and miscarriages and abortions.

Bereavement and grief over time

One major theme that is apparent through all these various sources is the very variable significance of time in the experiences of grief among young people. Some reactions to a death may be very overwhelming in the immediate aftermath and shock of the news. One-third of the callers to ChildLine called within two weeks of the death, with some calling from the hospital immediately after the death. But other aspects of bereavement may continue across the life course in the longer term.

We know very little about how grief is experienced over time, despite the well-worn reliance on the idea that 'time is a healer'. Morin and Welsh (1996), in their study of adolescent perceptions of death and bereavement in America, found that the most helpful coping strategy was the reminder that time would help. The least helpful were platitudes like, 'you'll get over it'.

Just how varied experiences can be, however, is shown by one contributor to the 'time-line' on the Cruse interactive website. Four years on from the death of her father, followed later by other family deaths, she wrote: 'the person that said time is a healer id like to meet and probably shoot because they obviously knew nothing! (Alison, http://www.rd4u.org.uk/person/years.html, accessed 11 July 2003, written as in the original). This is also apparent in the calls to ChildLine (Cross 2002).

Our three case studies, Shirleen, Neville and Brian, offer particular insights because these same individuals have been followed over several years. In this respect, Shirleen's responses to her great-grandfather's death can be seen to have perhaps mellowed a little over time, but the continuing – even increasing – vulnerability of Neville and Brian over many years is very striking. Furthermore, their stories show how ongoing issues, such as other losses, or anniversaries of the death, or the young person's own birthday, can trigger the grief felt immediately after the death.

Conclusions

Overall, there are a number of major issues that arise from our three case studies, alongside our review of other materials concerning the perspectives of young people:

- **The search for meaning** – Bereavement is an individual life event, which young people try to make sense of within the particular contexts of their own lives. Shirleen, Neville and Brian have each sought to make meaningful these events of life and death, and each attempts, at least at times, to consider the significance of bereavement for their view of life.
- **Overwhelming feelings** – Within this search for meaning, young people may struggle quite desperately to understand and cope with overwhelming and unexpected feelings following a deeply felt bereavement. At the same time, Shirleen is an important reminder that bereavements may be significant for young people without necessarily being experienced as a major disruption. In this regard, there may be many more 'voices' and experiences of young people in relation to bereavement that we have not yet heard.
- **Time** – Responses and interventions to bereavement may need to take a much longer time perspective than is currently the case, while people working with vulnerable young people generally need to be aware of the possibilities of such long-term implications of earlier bereavements. Earlier experiences may not always be 'in the past', and the associated emotions may be just beneath the surface.

- **Social relationships** – A major theme of all the varying accounts we have considered in this chapter has been the implications of bereavement for social relationships, with isolation sometimes occurring between family members. As Neville said in relation to his family relationships: 'Maybe the rest of them are just coping with it, or looking as if they're coping with it, but I'm not.'
- **Risk and vulnerability** – Sometimes, as the calls to ChildLine painfully demonstrate, family relationships can deteriorate to the point of outright abuse or neglect after a key bereavement. At the same time, young people's accounts also point to risks of social isolation, bullying and stigma outside family relationships. In a case such as Brian, an underlying vulnerability can be increased by bereavement, while Neville's story highlights how vulnerability may deepen over time.
- **Intervention with bereaved individuals** – None of our three case studies had had any particular intervention or opportunities for discussion of their bereavement provided to them, although we can also see their own efforts to 'cope'. Difficulties in social relationships, and lack of opportunities to talk, are major themes to emerge overall from this exploration of the 'voices' of young people. This raises issues about social attitudes generally towards bereavement, and the possibilities of educating young people in this area, both in relation to highly disruptive bereavements (such as Neville's) and other experiences of bereavement (such as Shirleen's). A range of bereavement experiences may constitute a feature of the life course of the great majority of young people (as we saw in the Introduction).
- **Referral processes** – Concerns about social isolation also point to the importance of referral processes available to young people, with or without their parents acting as gatekeepers to services and support.
- **Lack of power** – While the young people calling ChildLine were struggling to understand what they were feeling (Cross 2002), the research suggests that the feelings expressed are no different in kind to the sorts of feelings experienced by adults in similar circumstances. Instead, the differences centre more on the lack of power experienced by young people combined, frequently, with a sense of exclusion from decisions being made. Policy makers and practitioners need to include young people themselves more in decision making and information processes. It may be important for young people to feel that they have some input into the supports and services they may receive (Griffiths 2004; Hill 1999).

Many of these themes set the scene for much of this report, and will be considered further in the chapters that follow. But, overall, policy makers and practitioners, along with family members, friends and colleagues, need to be aware that grief may be unvoiced even while its impact is still being felt years after the death.

2. Constructing a knowledge base[1]

Introduction

In considering what is 'known' about young people and bereavement from the research literature, we have to explicitly consider that knowledge is never neutral: it is always framed within particular assumptions and developed using particular methodologies. In this chapter, we briefly consider some of the theories and methodologies that underpin the research evidence and literature that will be discussed in subsequent chapters, before explaining the approach taken in this project. Such discussion is essential if we are to be able to 'make sense' of the research evidence with all its complexities and contradictions. Different researchers have variable ideas about what are the important questions to ask, what is the most appropriate language to frame them, and what count as valid answers.

In considering the bereavement experiences of young people we may distinguish between:

1. bereavement as a pervasive experience in the lives of young people, that might be understood as a 'normal' part of 'growing up' (for example Shirleen's case study in Chapter 1); and
2. bereavement that has a significance for major emotional or biographical disruption, raising issues, perhaps, of increased vulnerability (for example Neville's case study), and sometimes for a changed identity or a sense of difference or stigma.

The research and professional literature has focused overwhelmingly on the latter experience, but this in itself may help to construct and reinforce ideas of bereavement and death as something 'apart' from 'normal' life and experience, that requires 'expert' knowledge to understand it. Such continuities and discontinuities

1 We wish to acknowledge the particular input of earlier working papers written by Wendy Martin that underpin sections of this chapter.

in the research literature then *inter*-relate in important ways with the ways in which professional specialisms and services may develop, leaving other general services for young people feeling that they lack 'expertise' in dealing with bereavement. Such issues have been discussed by some social science theorists.

Theorising young people and bereavement

The historical processes of western societies, discussed briefly in the Introduction, which led to the 'public absence/private presence' of death, have arguably led to a view of bereavement and grief as primarily individualised, 'internal' experiences (Small and Hockey 2001). This view removes bereavement and grief from their social context, and has led to a view of death and dying as the province of specialists, whose expertise is rationalised, medicalised and secularised (Field 1996; Hockey 1996).

Such historical developments culminated in new debates about how to manage death in the mid-twentieth century, leading to a significant growth in the literature theorising loss and bereavement. (Details of the various models of how ('normal'/'healthy', and 'pathological'/'unhealthy') grief is experienced are outlined in the Ribbens McCarthy 2006, forthcoming). But these various theories of grief may or may not resonate with ordinary people's everyday experiences of bereavement in daily life and how they manage grief in various social contexts (Walter 1999). As researchers, we need to know whether there is a satisfactory empirical base for the development of bereavement models that have been so widely used and applied. It is also important for policy makers and practitioners to have some understanding of the theories and debates behind bereavement counselling as they provide an assumed framework for what is considered good practice.

Many professionals appear to have embraced psychological theories of bereavement and grief processes, perhaps as a way of making some sense of the chaos of bereavement in the context of a largely secular society (Walter 1999). They have incorporated and institutionalised these theories into professional practices and training, which then become prescriptions for interventions (Small and Hockey 2001), which may then be challenged in their turn.

In the context of the psychological and therapeutic literature on bereavement and young people, the work of Fleming and colleagues (Fleming and Adolph 1986; Fleming and Balmer 1996) is now widely cited as providing the most relevant theoretical framework. In this model, 'adolescence' is a key concept, defined as ages 11 to 21, and divided into three periods with specific tasks and conflicts.

Bereavement is seen as interfering with this 'natural progression'. Adjustment to death, it is argued, will partly reflect the developmental task that was being faced at the time of the death.

Such developmental theories of adolescence point to various issues in relation to bereavement (Balk 1995), including:

- particular ambivalences around relationships, including the urge for autonomy (Raphael 1984)
- developments in cognitive capacities
- identify formation
- a heightened risk of psychopathology, associated with the 'storm and stress' of adolescence (Beratis 1991).

In line with the psychological underpinnings of the bereavement literature generally (discussed further later), this psychologically and biologically based theoretical framework of 'adolescence' (Gillies 2000) is heavily predominant in the specialist literature that considers bereavement in relation to young people, including the great majority of research studies in this area.

Sociological or social policy perspectives on youth view the teenage years through a different theoretical lens, as a transitional and relational age status that is socially constructed, and that carries implications for relative powerlessness and social vulnerability (for example, Brannen and others 2002; Furlong and Cartmel 1997; Jones and Wallace 1992; Wyn and White 1997). There is considerable untapped potential to build on those alternative theoretical approaches to consider how bereavement may be understood from these rather different vantage points.

Teenagers in western societies are moving from childhood non-responsibility to a position of responsibility via self-control (Ribbens McCarthy and Edwards 2000). Taking drugs or drinking, for example, can be seen as a way of resisting self-control and responsibility for one's own body. Young people may be exploring the limits, possibilities, advantages and disadvantages of (loss of) control of the body, and this may have particular implications for young people's understanding of death, since death so centrally and inescapably focuses our attention on the significance of bodies.

Youth culture and consumerism have been particular features of sociological research on young people, and are argued to have led to a celebration of youth, and the body beautiful (Featherstone 1995). Consequently: '"Youth" now has symbolic value as the "outcome" of the process of becoming more and more in control over one's body' (Wyn and White 1997: 20).

In various ways, then, young people may be seen to be 'testing out' the limits of reality and the possible consequences (Holland 2002). In this context, death may thus be seen as particularly shocking, and as an inappropriate intrusion, a death 'out of time'.

Some common concepts seem to occur in the separate literatures of 'bereavement' and 'youth', particularly those of 'transition' and the potential for 'disruption'. This is a striking coincidence, and raises questions about whether the conjunction of bereavement and youth may be regarded as particularly risky and difficult, since both may involve very significant change (transitions) and may involve threats to existing order (disruptions). Such variations in the theoretical and conceptual basis for understanding bereavement and young people then interrelate with variations in methodological approaches.

Methodological issues

In Chapter 1, we briefly overviewed the available qualitative literature providing evidence of young people's perspectives on bereavement. In relation to this sort of evidence, we mentioned key considerations about the characteristics of those whose 'voices' are heard, and the part played by the researcher in the joint construction of the resulting research account. Furthermore, there may be enormous variation in the interpretive framework used to analyse and present such qualitative evidence. Qualitative evidence generally may be rooted, for example, in a clinical or therapeutic perspective, an ethnographic approach, a narrative analysis, an interventionist 'helping' perspective (whether autobiographically or professionally based), or a psychological, developmental theoretical base. Many of these established general approaches to qualitative research, however, hardly appear at all in the literature on bereavement and young people.

By contrast, the vast majority of relevant specialist literature uses more structured, quantitative methodologies, although here again, there may be an array of disciplinary and theoretical underpinnings to such work. There are three main research approaches that provide quantitative evidence concerning bereavement and young people:

1. Research that analyses information about young people who have been randomly selected from the population of young people generally. This includes longitudinal and cohort studies which can be used to investigate whether there is a statistically significant association between particular (undesirable) outcomes and the occurrence of bereavement, generally focused exclusively on parental deaths.

2. Research that identifies young people who are known to have been bereaved, and considers the incidence of particular effects for these young people, ideally with a control group for comparison.
3. Research that considers young people who have been identified as having manifested problematic outcomes in their lives, and then looks back to see if there is a higher incidence of prior bereavement than would be expected from what is known about young people generally. This is a fairly small body of literature.

The great majority of the studies that we accessed in this literature search fall into the second approach, and these are overwhelmingly medical or psychological in their theoretical underpinnings, and largely based on research in the USA.

Causality and 'risk'

Besides trying to establish descriptive statistics (such as the prevalence rates discussed in the Introduction), most of these studies seek to establish some sort of causal connection between the earlier experience of bereavement and later outcomes. However, there are complex issues about how to infer 'causality' in these various literatures (Ribbens McCarthy 2006, forthcoming).

There are also further theoretical issues in terms of how we may understand 'risk' in relation to particular outcomes in an individual's life. In the current UK social policy context, risk is understood as a factor whose presence can increase vulnerability to features of social exclusion, or whose absence can protect against social exclusion (Bynner 2001).

In the context of bereavement, statistical patterns and associations may be particularly difficult to establish and interpret for causal relationships, given the fact that bereavement may have opposite effects for different individuals. Consequently, different individual 'effects' may cancel each other out in the analyses of large data sets. Further issues concern which outcomes to study, and the timing at which an 'outcome' is measured – since outcomes may fluctuate or show delayed effects.

Longitudinal and cohort studies

Much UK literature relies on the longitudinal and cohort studies (for further details see http://www.cls.ioe.ac.uk/) referred to earlier in the first category. Indeed, the UK has a strong reputation for this type of general study of the lives of large numbers of children over time. These data sets may hold highly relevant information about children who have lost a parent through death, but they vary greatly in the ways in which they classify these children – often subsuming them within an overall category of children who come from 'broken homes'. Furthermore, where bereaved children are classified in their own right, low numbers in the 'parental death' category can mean that even quite large differences may not reach statistically significant levels (Sweeting and others 1998). The strength of these studies, however, rests on the fact that many of the longitudinal studies followed the same individuals over decades, providing reasonably strong grounds for deriving causal explanations over time, though this is a complex issue (Ribbens McCarthy 2006, forthcoming).

Eminent researchers who have drawn on these data bases to provide evidence concerning bereaved children and young people include, for example, Douglas (1970); Douglas and others (1968); Elliott and others (1993); Buchanan and Brinke (1997); Maclean and Kuh (1991); Schoon and Montgomery (1997); Schoon and Parsons (2002); and Wadsworth (1979, 1984, 1991). It is crucial to note, however, that most of the literature here is not focused on questions about bereavement as such, but on factors such as divorce. Where analyses about bereaved children are included in this literature, this is often in terms of what light they may shed on issues about divorce. As a result, it is perhaps not surprising that the evidence concerning the significance of the death of a parent may sometimes be subject to simplistic generalisations. But it is all too easy for such generalisations to gain the status of a kind of lay or mythological 'expert' truth.

Quantitative studies of bereaved young people

In relation to studies of young people known to have been bereaved, there are also major methodological weaknesses to consider, particularly in relation to the nature of the samples studied, in terms of both how they are accessed and who is willing to talk about bereavement to researchers – which is itself likely to reflect the extent to which they see talk as useful. The absence of control groups is another widespread weakness of these studies. The Childhood Bereavement Study in Boston, USA (Worden 1996) is particularly noteworthy for being more robust than most, involving 70 families (120 children), accessed through general community based services such as funeral parlours, selected prior to any referral for counselling, and interviewed at four months, one year and two years after the death of a parent. Control groups were also included. The research instruments involved a variety of psychological adjustment scores, but also more qualitative insights. The study was, however, limited to one particular type of locality, and replications are needed in other areas and other societies.

Societal and social contexts

In the UK, however, there has been no study similar to that of Worden (1996), leaving us heavily reliant on research from the USA. American research includes both longitudinal and community based research, such as the work of Balk (1991, 1995, 2000); Balk and Corr (1996); Fleming and Adolph (1986); Fleming and Balmer (1996); Gersten and others (1991); Mack (2001); Worden (1996); and Worden, Davies and McCown (1999). Often, however, there is little dialogue between these different literatures, and very little discussion of the local social, or larger societal, contexts in which these studies are embedded (as discussed in the Introduction and Chapter 1). There is also a small amount of research based in other countries, such as Greece, Australia and Israel, the latter particularly perhaps raising issues about different social, cultural and religious contexts for young people's experiences of bereavement. These issues of the broader societal context need to be held in mind when considering the evidence presented in the following chapters.

Generally, there is a real paucity of UK research focused specifically on bereavement and young people, with some noteworthy exceptions (for example Black 1991; Cross 2002; Harrison and Harrington 2001). UK writers have, however, been very important in developing theoretical perspectives, in both sociological and clinical literatures.

The methodology of the literature review

It will be apparent, then, that the range of literatures potentially relevant to our topic is vast, highly variable, and often both theoretically and methodologically contentious. These were important considerations in how we set about the review. And, indeed, our own decision making and writing around this review is clearly rooted in our[2] own backgrounds as family and medical sociologists.

The remit for the literature review was to focus on young people specifically. We adopted a wide definition of the term 'young people', to refer to the teenage years and the early 20s. But the conjoining of 'bereavement' and 'young people' can implicate quite different time trajectories. We had to recognise that:

- on the one hand, we might risk a somewhat arbitrary and artificial slicing of the research literature available

---

2 The project team overall has, at various points, included Julie Jessop, Wendy Martin, Jane Ribbens McCarthy and Sue Sharpe.

- on the other hand, we needed to keep open a theoretical and empirical space for considering whether the teenage years do indeed raise particular issues for experiences of bereavement.

We also knew that the term 'young people' is one that is particularly relevant to policy and sociological literatures, while the more psychologically based literatures tend to use the term 'adolescence'. Similarly, we knew that the concept 'loss' would potentially cover an enormous array of literatures. We therefore began our searches using a carefully selected set of key terms, namely: adolescence; young people; teenager; young adult; youth *and* grief; mourning; bereavement.

However, it soon became clear that the concept of 'bereavement' is very heavily based in a psychological/therapeutic/medical theoretical framework and in professional practices. As a term, it is rarely used by sociologists or other academic social researchers (with some notable exceptions, such as Riches and Dawson 2000; Small and Hockey 2001; Walter 1999). And much of the work that was indeed about young people was embedded within theories and research samples that were framed by reference to children generally. In our later searches, therefore, we extended our terms to include children, death, dying and loss. These terms did lead us to other areas of literature but, as anticipated, the extent of the literature uncovered became very difficult to manage. We supplemented these systematic searches with information and publications recommended by key researchers and professionals.

Conclusions

The knowledge base available concerning bereavement and young people is shaped by its theoretical underpinnings and methodological approaches. There is a strong imbalance in the existing literature between sociology (of the socio-historical contexts, understandings of death and dying, and youth), and psychology (of bereavement and loss, including adolescent bereavement). This current predominance of psychological perspectives around bereavement and young people raises questions about whether this in itself reflects the individualisation of grief and the sequestration of experience in contemporary western societies.

There is a clear need for dialogue between these literatures, and for theoretical frameworks that are able to cross the disciplinary divides (Ribbens McCarthy 2006, forthcoming).

The research evidence that we go on to examine has to be understood in the social context of its production, including its chosen theoretical and methodological frameworks.

3. Is bereavement a 'risk factor' in young people's lives?

Introduction

The major focus of the research evidence relating to young people and bereavement concerns deaths that might be expected to constitute a major disruption in a child or young person's life, particularly the death of a parent and, to a lesser extent, the death of a sibling. This research has used largely quantitative, structured methodologies to ask whether such bereavement may be associated with particular sorts of outcomes for young people's lives, particularly outcomes that might be considered to be undesirable and disadvantageous. In this sense, they focus on the question of whether bereavement may be seen to constitute, to a degree that is manifest through statistical significance, a 'risk' factor in young people's lives.

In the previous chapter we briefly outlined three ways in which researchers might develop empirical answers to such a question, drawing on different sorts of samples and variable theoretical frameworks. If each of these approaches found bereavement to be significant for life chances, then we would have a strong framework for regarding it as a key overall risk factor in the lives of young people.

Unfortunately, however, as will become apparent in this chapter, the evidence available does not lead to any such clarity of conclusions, although it does point to some important findings of outcomes and experiences that are clearly highly significant in the lives of the young people studied. In this chapter we briefly review some of the main themes covered in this complex literature; further details of the research findings that underpin the following discussion are available in the book (Ribbens McCarthy 2006, forthcoming).

We first consider studies which largely focus on issues of bereaved individuals' social adjustment, particularly drawing on the longitudinal and cohort studies of large numbers of young people generally, before turning to studies that are more focused on issues of mental health and psychological adjustment, largely from a psychological or medical perspective, using samples of young people known to have been bereaved. We then explore some of the issues – beyond those of the bereavement per se – that may need to be taken into account in order to understand some of the complexities of what is happening in the statistical data, before developing a discussion that seeks to draw out some of the conclusions that may be made on the basis of this variety of evidence.

Aspects of social adjustment

One of the comments often made about children who have been bereaved, is that they have had to 'grow up too fast'. We examined how true this was in relation to key markers of transitions to adulthood, based on the available quantitative research data.

Education

Some research suggests that children's concentration at school may be affected by parental bereavement (for example Worden 1996), but the evidence regarding the relevance of parental bereavement on educational qualifications, school leaving, and entry into labour markets is both contradictory and complex, with interactions apparent at times in relation to gender and also social class (for example Maclean and Kuh 1991).

Dowdney's review of the evidence (2000) concludes that educational performance and age of completion of education may be affected by parental bereavement, but this may vary between individual children. Furthermore, other circumstances may be relevant, such as whether or not the death was preceded by a long illness (Douglas and others 1968). In some cases (as we saw with both Neville and Brian in Chapter 1), the young person will want to try harder for the sake of their dead parent, while in others it will have a negative impact. Furthermore, the implications of bereavement may not occur evenly across all areas of the school curriculum (Elliot and others 1993), and may fluctuate over time (Sweeting and others 1998) (as we saw in the case of Neville). One study also found an association between parental death and longer-term unemployment among men (Maclean and Wadsworth 1988).

Leaving home early

Only one study, in the UK (Kiernan 1992), has considered whether parental bereavement is associated with leaving home early. This study used data from the National Child Development Study to consider a range of 'transitions' for young people in relation to parental bereavement. In this analysis, leaving home early was the one area where there was found to be a particular, statistically significant, positive association with parental death.

Early sexual activity and partnering

The study by Kiernan (1992) did not find any evidence that loss of a parent through death was associated with early partnering, sexual activities or parenthood. This contrasts markedly with the finding from a Scottish study (Sweeting and others 1998), that girls whose parent had died were the most likely of all groups to be engaged in early sexual activities and were eight times more likely to be pregnant at age 18 than those living with both birth parents. This is in line with an earlier study based on the 1946 UK cohort (Douglas 1970).

The question of early partnering is another area, however, where different individuals may show contradictory tendencies. Tyson-Rawson's (1996) smaller, in-depth study in the USA found that paternally bereaved young women tended to polarise, either moving quickly into committed relationships or avoiding them altogether. There are some suggestions from the clinical literature (Raphael 1984) that paternal bereavement may be associated with a fear of close relationships. These findings together are suggestive that parental bereavement may have some implications for early sexual activity and partnering, but these may occur in contradictory ways for different individuals.

Criminal or disruptive behaviours

Various studies have considered whether bereavement is associated with behaviours that are criminal or disruptive in some other way. One community based study (Sweeting and others 1998), for example, found that young women whose parents had died were more likely than any other group examined in their study to be engaging in poor *health behaviours* when studied during their teenage years (smoking, drinking, drugs). Again, the clinical literature also suggests that such behaviours may be found among bereaved young people of either sex (Raphael 1984; and see discussion in Brown 2002).

In relation to *disruptive behaviours*, some studies (Elliott and others 1993; Worden 1996) do point to higher levels than expected of aggressive or disruptive behaviours among parentally bereaved children. Others, however, (Gersten and others 1991) have not found any link between parental bereavement and conduct disorder, while Rutter and others (1998) conclude that there is only a 'minimal' association between parental death and risk of antisocial behaviour.

It is important, however, to distinguish between research concerned with disruptive behaviour and that concerned with criminal behaviour. With respect to studies of young people who have been formally *convicted of offences*, there has been a long history of research (dating back to the 1920s) that has considered whether or not there may be a link between 'broken homes' and delinquency (McCord 1982). However, not only is this literature very confusing and uncertain about what conclusions can be drawn about this topic as a whole (Loeber and Dishion 1983), it is also particularly confusing about the significance of homes 'broken' by parental death as one aspect of this body of work (Ribbens McCarthy 2006, forthcoming).

In Farrington's (1996) review of the literature on youth offending, the different types of 'broken homes' are not always distinguished in the studies that he discusses, but where the cause of the break is considered, parental death generally appears not to be significant for offending behaviour. Wells and Rankin (1991), however, in their review and meta-analysis of a great range of such studies, conclude that *both* delinquency and divorce/separation on the one hand, and delinquency and parental death on the other, show similar levels of being associated variables.

Among those working in the criminal justice system with young offenders, bereavement also has a long history of being identified as a background feature of criminal behaviour (for example Allen, Sprigings and Kyng 2003; Boswell 1996; Finlay and Jones 2000; Liddle and Solanki 2002; Shoor and Speed 1963), particularly if drug related or involving more serious crimes. Few of these studies, however, use prevalence figures (as discussed in our Introduction) to consider whether the rates of bereavement found among these offenders are higher than might be expected among a general population of young people – a serious methodological weakness. Nevertheless, some of them identify somewhat higher levels than might be expected generally (for example Boswell (1996) found that 10 per cent of the serious offenders studied had experienced the death of a parent), while others point to bereavement as an important feature in either the professionals' or young people's perceptions of their personal, mental and criminal histories.

Discussion of this issue needs to distinguish more carefully between different sorts of aggressive, disruptive and more serious criminal behaviours, as well as different reasons for loss of contact with parents. There is some evidence supporting the idea that bereavement may be a risk factor for offending behaviour, particularly if drug related or for more serious crimes.

Aspects of mental health and psychological adjustment

In relation to various health outcomes, firm conclusions are elusive, given the methodological complexities and frequent weaknesses in research design (Ribbens McCarthy 2006, forthcoming).

Depression and general mental health risks

There have been suggestions (Goodyer 1995) that bereavement may be a life event that is associated with depression in particular, rather than other forms of psychiatric risk. However, there is uncertainty and controversy in the literature over whether bereavement is likely to lead to increased risk of depression, either in the short or long term. Furthermore, definitions of depression and distress differ, along with assessment of their implications: 'painful reflections on a difficult past are not the same as an inability to feel and function competently in the present' (Kelly 2003: 249).

Harrington and Harrison's (1999) discussion particularly argues against any automatic assumption that bereavement is associated with a risk of mental health issues. This might indicate that we should be careful not to expect that all bereaved adolescents will necessarily experience deep grief and emotional reactions to bereavement, but nonetheless it could still be an important issue for a considerable minority even where this does not amount to clinically defined mental illness.

Nevertheless, many of the studies of parental or sibling bereavement (Agid and others 1999; Balmer 1992, discussed in Fleming and Balmer 1996; Berney and others 1991, discussed in Goodyer 1995; Birtchnell 1972; Black 1978, 1993a; Brent and others 1993; Harrison and Harrington 2001; Hogan and DeSantis 1994; Mack 2001; Meltzer and others 2000; Servaty and Hayslip 2001; Wadsworth 1991; Worden 1996; Worden, Davies and McCown 1999; Zall 1994), though not all (Canetti and others 2000; Kendler and others 1992; Maclean and Wadsworth 1988; Schoon and Montgomery 1997) find some link with depression, both in the teenage years and more long term. Some studies clearly point to parental bereavement as a risk factor in epidemiological terms (Gersten and others 1991). Dowdney, in a review of the literature concerning parental death specifically, suggests that:

> ... children do experience grief, sadness and despair following parental death. Mild depression is frequent. However, when clinically referred children are excluded, psychiatric disorder characterises only a very small minority of children ... Most commonly, bereaved children present with a wide range of emotional and behavioural symptoms that constitute a nonspecific disturbance ... One in five is likely to manifest such disturbance at a level sufficient to justify referral to specialist services.
> *(2000: 827–28)*

The long-term issues are especially difficult to establish, and the findings are complex and contradictory. There are particular methodological difficulties in longitudinal studies of depression, not least the question of the variability (Lowton and Higginson 2002), and adequacy (Harrington and Vostanis 1995) of measuring instruments available. While some studies point to the persistence of, or even increase in, depressive symptoms over time, the longer-term implications may be particularly overlooked. And yet: 'There are still many questions regarding why it is that some individuals are resilient while others are vulnerable and go on to develop long-term problems' (Worden 1996: 105).

Professionals need to be aware that bereavement may have both ongoing and longer-term implications in the lives of young people. They may be unaware of earlier bereavements in the young person's life, or there may be an (unfounded) expectation that the significance of such losses may have subsided. As we saw with Neville (in Chapter 1), this may be far from the reality.

Self-concept and more 'positive' outcomes

As we discussed in the Introduction, not all outcomes from bereavement experiences need necessarily be regarded as unequivocally negative. There may, for example, be scope for individuals to gain a different – perhaps more realistic – perspective on life, or a sense of increased strength or maturity in the face of adversity, to develop more spiritual beliefs or a deeper appreciation of the value of their significant relationships – as when Shirleen (in Chapter 1) took care to spend time with her grandparents after the death of her great-grandfather. More prosaically, individuals may benefit from the ending of a conflict-ridden or abusive relationship.

Balk (1995) in particular has paid this issue considerable attention, in relation to American adolescents bereaved of a sibling. He found that such young people either came close to, or had better, scores on psychological scales measuring positive self-concept when compared with other adolescents. Such higher self-concept scores have been found to occur even seven or nine years after the death (Martinson and others 1987, discussed by Hogan and DeSantis 1994). However, Balk (1995) also found great variation around this issue, alongside reports of continued confusion, suicidal thoughts, fearfulness and eating difficulties among some individuals.

In contrast, Worden's work (1996) found that parentally bereaved children believed they were less able to effect change than their non-bereaved counterparts. By the second anniversary of the death, bereaved children reported significantly lower self-worth than the control group. Tyson-Rawson, also discussing parentally bereaved adolescents, refers to 'the opportunity inherent in crisis [to] give rise to a stronger sense of self and the value of others' (1996: 158), although her own work suggests they may feel more vulnerable and less in control.

It may be that some parental deaths in particular have a major impact on young people's life experiences, especially if the death results in other life changes, in ways that may not be found to be so widespread in relation to sibling deaths, which then undermine the individual's self-concept and sense of control. Again, however, complexity must be acknowledged. For example, Worden, Davies and McCown (1999) found that boys and girls differed with respect to their reactions to parent or sibling loss (although the implications for self-esteem were not directly considered).

The evidence from these studies thus suggests that parental and sibling bereavement may have different implications for self-esteem. It is important that interventions remain open to the possibility that significant bereavements can sometimes have ambivalent, or even positive, effects, with consequences for young people's approach to life.

Developing more complex understandings

More recent quantitative studies have sought to develop more sophisticated statistical analyses to unravel some of the complexities and contradictions found in earlier studies of outcomes for children and young people, around concepts of both risk and resilience (Amato 2000; Haggerty 1994; Luthar, Cicchetti and Becker 2000; Rutter 1999; Schoon and Parsons 2002). While these studies tend to centre on divorce or potential sources of developmental psychopathology in children's lives, these approaches may provide useful theoretical models in relation to bereavement as well. A variety of cross-cutting variables may thus underlay some of the complexities and contradictions in the findings discussed earlier. These may be understood in terms of individual differences, family relationships and aspects of social structure.

Individual differences

We have suggested throughout this report so far that the significance of a particular category of bereavement may depend very much on the meaning the death holds for the individual concerned. In understanding statistical patterns in large data sets, it is difficult to take account of how young people themselves frame and understand a bereavement, but this factor may help to account for the ways in which opposite changes seem to occur between different bereaved individuals. For example, religious beliefs may both shape, and be shaped by, bereavement experiences (Balk 1991; Hogan and DeSantis 1994), although here again the evidence is complex (Ringler and Hayden 2000). As Rutter comments, in his discussion of psychosocial research generally: 'It has been crucially important to appreciate that the risk derives as much from the meaning attributed to the event as from objective qualities of the event itself' (2000: 390).

Some psychologists have studied the relevance of personality factors for bereavement outcomes, which have been suggested to affect the individual's adjustment to loss (Balmer 1992, reported in Fleming and Balmer 1996). Coping style may vary between individuals, and between genders, and has been found to be important in dealing with life stressors more generally. Age 15 has been identified as a time when young people 'encounter a turning point in the use of more efficacious and adaptive strategies in dealing with stress' (Seiffge-Krenke 2000: 677).

Family relationships

The levels of conflict and other family processes that occurred between parents prior to divorce have been identified as important for children's functioning after divorce (Amato 2000; Amato and Booth 1996, cited in Sweeting and others 1998; Hetherington 2003). It would seem that similar experiences concerning the nature of relationships *prior* to bereavement may affect the way a young person deals with a parent's death (Douglas and others 1968).

Pervasive findings point to the relevance of parental conflict for children's well-being (Amato 1993, 2000; Rodgers and Pryor 1998), and Sweeting and others (1998) found that bereaved teenagers were as likely as separated families to have been experiencing parental conflict. This does point to a possibility that for some bereaved children, the death of a parent could actually improve their life situation if it leads to a final resolution of overt parental conflict.

Alternatively, grieving may be affected if the attachment was complex. Worden (1996) found that the pre-death relationship between a child or young person and a parent who died mediated some of the impact of the bereavement, especially the level of ambivalence.

Other issues concern the nature of relationships *after* the death of a family member. In a single-parent household, the presence of only one parent may reduce the amount of time available for family activities, and this may have implications for well-being (Amato 1993; Sweeting and others 1998; discussed further in Ribbens McCarthy 2006, forthcoming). Furthermore, it might be expected that a major family bereavement, such as a parent or child, might lead any surviving parent(s) to be less emotionally available to support their (surviving) children. It is widely argued, for example, that widow(er)s are at risk of poor physical and mental health (Gersten and others 1991; Parkes 1998; Worden 1996), although Mack (2001) found that parental death was not followed by a poorer quality relationship with the surviving parent.

It is clear that relationships with surviving family members can be experienced as problematic after bereavement: people may, for example, strive for 'mutual protection' or may impose particular expectations on children and young people (Clark and others 1994; Demi and Gilbert 1987; Sutcliffe and others 1998; Worden 1996; and see our earlier case study of Neville). Family relationships may also deteriorate to a point of 'extreme alienation' (Gray 1989) or outright abuse (Cross 2002).

On the other hand, family relationships may be experienced as very supportive, and several studies point to the significance of the well-being and 'competence' of survivors (Black 2002; Fleming and Balmer 1996; Gersten and others 1991; Gray 1989; Tyson-Rawson 1996; Worden 1996;). Parental relationships characterised as warm, empathetic or close have been found to be associated with more favourable emotional reports from surviving children, in both the short- and long-term (Guerriero and Fleming 1985, discussed in Balk 1995; Saler and Skolnick 1992). In a later discussion, Fleming and Balmer review evidence about family support, which could sometimes be conflicting, but conclude that a 'bereaved adolescent could view the family environment as helpful in adjusting to death if that family unit is cohesive, allows for members to express opinions, and is low in conflict' (1996: 147).

The remarriage or repartnering of the surviving parent after a parental bereavement is mentioned as an issue in some studies but, again, the evidence is confusing. Worden (1996) actually found that this seemed to reduce children's anxiety levels and concerns about the safety of the surviving parent.

Features of social structure: class, race and gender

As noted in the Introduction, parental bereavement rates are likely to vary between different social groups, pointing to the relevance of social structure. Additionally, social class and material circumstances are significant issues in the pattern of outcomes associated with bereavement and parental death (Harrison and Harrington 2001; Worden 1996), although social class effects may also differ between the sexes (Elliott and others 1993; Maclean and Kuh 1991).

Paternal death, particularly, may have implications for material well-being (Elliott and others 1993), which vary with social class, and affluence appears to mitigate some of the outcomes of parental death (see Ribbens McCarthy 2006, forthcoming). The relationship between material circumstances and subsequent disruptions and changes may also be important for outcomes (Harrison and Harrington 2001; Worden 1996).

The ways in which race interrelates with class and material circumstances has not received attention within the empirical literature – not even in relation to divorce (Amato 2000). But minority ethnic groups may already have experienced significant losses of various kinds in their lives, through experiences of migration, disadvantage and racism, which may increase their vulnerability when dealing with the loss of bereavement (Desai and Bevan 2002). This is important in the context of other evidence showing that there may be increased risks in relation to bereavement outcomes if an individual has also experienced increased vulnerability for other reasons, or additional losses (this is discussed further later).

Gender has been clearly shown to make a considerable difference to experiences of parental bereavement, both in terms of the child concerned, and in terms of the surviving parent (Black 1993a; Douglas 1970; Kiernan 1992; Maclean and Kuh 1991; Sweeting and others 1998; Worden 1996). There is also some evidence of gender differences in reactions to the death of a sibling (Balmer 1992, reported in Fleming and Balmer 1996; Guerriero and Fleming 1985, discussed by Balk 1995; Worden,

Davies and McCown 1999). There have also been many suggestions over the years that it may be more disruptive of everyday life if it is the mother rather than the father who has died (Tyson-Rawson 1996; Worden 1996, and see the discussion of Cross (2002) in Chapter 1), and this links to wider evidence concerning the significance of mothers for the family lives of teenagers generally (Brannen and others 1994; Gillies, Ribbens McCarthy and Holland 2001; Langford and others 2001). Some suggest that maternal death signifies a greater risk factor than paternal death for adult outcomes such as depression (Dowdney 2000) but paternal death may have more implications for material circumstances.

Additionally, with regard to these different individual, family and structural variables overall, there may be also complex *interactions* between different factors here. For example, Worden (1996) found that the 'dysfunction' of the surviving parent (particularly in terms of a 'passive' rather than an 'active' coping style) was an important mediator of the consequences of children's experiences of parental death. This dysfunction consistently put the children at risk, he concluded. But other factors may also be seen to come into play in accounting for such differences in a parent's 'functioning', since a passive coping style was itself associated with a variety of other difficulties experienced by the household, which themselves relate to features of social structure, such as class, ethnicity and material circumstances.

Such interwoven factors of individual differences, family relationships and features of social structure appear to have a considerable bearing on the outcomes for bereaved young people. These issues may mediate the 'risks' or likelihood of bereavement leading to particular 'effects', cautioning against any simplistic generalisations about links between a particular event (bereavement) or household type (for example a widowed single parent) and specific outcomes. They may also help to account for apparently opposite 'effects' between different individuals. The general failure to take account of these factors may well account for the multiplicity of contradictory findings in this area.

Conclusions

In this chapter, we have particularly explored evidence from quantitatively based research studies focused largely on parental and (to a lesser extent) sibling bereavement, in relation to a limited range of social and general mental health outcomes among young people, sometimes extending into their adult lives. We have not considered the implications for physical health, or specific mental health issues such as eating disorders. Nor have we considered studies that look at particular causes of death: bereavement as a result of suicide or other traumatic death, for example, may carry different implications than deaths that were preceded by a long illness. (References on these topics are available on request from the authors, who can be contacted by email: J.C.Ribbens-Mccarthy@open.ac.uk.)

The studies we have discussed are equivocal, sometimes leading to fierce debates about their implications. The confusion and inconsistencies in the literature are very striking. Taken together, however, they suggest that there can be important negative (and sometimes positive) outcomes for some bereaved children, but that these may depend on the nature of the bereavement, how the individual experiences it, and also the presence of other factors, such as the nature of the previous relationship with the deceased person, or the level of material resources to help provide continuing stability in other areas of everyday life.

In relation to aspects of social adjustment, while inconclusive and inconsistent, the evidence shows that bereavement may carry implications for educational and learning processes and outcomes, for early home leaving, for early sexual activities and poor health behaviours, and possibly for aggressive or delinquent behaviours.

Evidence concerning mental health and psychological adjustment following parental or sibling death certainly points to high levels of short-term distress and depressive symptoms for large numbers – but by no means all – of young people who experience such bereavement in their lives. And while some may demonstrate enhanced self-worth and express a sense of increased maturity as a result of bereavement experiences, others appear to be at risk of reduced self-esteem, particularly where parental death is associated with a considerable number of life changes.

One particularly noteworthy feature of the literature concerns the possibility – even the likelihood – that children and young people may continue to feel the consequences of a significant bereavement over the years of their young lives. The implications for their adult lives are even more difficult to establish, but again there is evidence of long-term risks for some young people, especially in conjunction with other difficult issues in their lives. Some evidence suggests, for example, that parentally bereaved children are at greater risk of experiencing depression as adults, although the underlying patterns may be complex. There may well be a need to consider whether responses to bereavement need to take a much longer time perspective.

Yet bereavement as a single event may not in itself increase the risk of negative outcomes for the young person, particularly where other life circumstances – such as material affluence and positive family relationships – are favourable. However, the way in which bereavement features within the individual's life course more broadly, or in the context of other life circumstances, may indeed be associated with increased risk.

Studies of bereavement and depression, for example, suggest that adolescents who experience more than one significant bereavement are at greater risk of depression (Harrison and Harrington 2001). The level of risk for undesirable outcomes has been shown to be high for those individuals who experience multiple disadvantages generally (Carron and Rutter 1991, cited by Seiffge-Krenke 2000; Harrison and Harrington 2001; Rodgers 1990) or multiple problematic life events (Gersten and others 1991; Meltzer and others 2000). For example, high scores on emotional distress among young people generally may be the result of:

> ... a series or chain of problems ... [in which] one precipitated the another, and ... social and family circumstances and self-esteem were not strong enough to support the individual at such times ... Thus, adult vulnerability to emotional difficulties may be the current end point of many earlier experiences of problems, some a matter of bad luck, some a question of self-regard, and others a problem of poor social support; the many interrelationships found between these factors add to the likelihood of strong links perpetuating the chain over many years.
> *(Wadsworth 1991: 140–41)*

As the calls to ChildLine reveal (Cross 2002, discussed in Chapter 1), bereavement itself may also render children more vulnerable to other risks. Nevertheless, as Dowdney (2000: 823) points out: 'Although it is tempting to ponder the possibility that parental death increases child vulnerability to later stressors or loss, this hypothesis has never been tested'.

The evidence available from the literature on bereavement and young people supports the need for more complex explanatory models such as those advocated by Amato (2000), Schoon and Parsons (2002) and Thompson (2002), concerning the ways in which major family events may be experienced. Schoon and Parsons argue for models that can include:

- characteristics of the children themselves
- features of their families
- aspects of their wider social contexts.

Amato (2000), writing in the relation to issues of divorce, suggests the need for models that can view the divorce as a process rather than an event, associated with 'mediators' (stressors) and 'moderators' (protective factors), leading to varied aspects of 'adjustment'. Certainly the evidence presented earlier supports the need to take account of all these issues. Simplistic generalisations are unlikely to further such understandings, and there is a clear need for more sophisticated statistical analyses, focused specifically on issues of bereavement in their own right, and using robust research designs with adequate samples of large numbers of young people. There is also a pressing need for real dialogue between the literature based on the longitudinal studies of general populations of young people and the more medically oriented literature based on samples of bereaved young people.

Overall, then, this review of the quantitative research points towards similar conclusions to the review of the more qualitative research (Chapter 1). Policy makers and practitioners need to be aware that for all young people experiencing a significant bereavement there is the potential for both short- and long-term consequences, particularly where general resources (personal, social and material) are low, or other stressors are high. Bereavement may also be a potentially relevant issue to consider when helping particularly troubled and vulnerable young people (Barry, 2001; Johnston and others, 2000). At the same time, we also need to be aware that some young people may not show any particularly negative effects. The implications of these conclusions will be pursued further in subsequent chapters.

4. The social contexts of bereavement experiences and interventions

By Julie Jessop and Jane Ribbens McCarthy

Bereavement as a public and private issue

In Chapter 3, we considered bereavement in terms of its significance in the lives of young people viewed largely in individual terms. But the death of a family member or significant other, while often a deeply personal experience, has to be dealt with in a variety of social contexts and institutional settings. In this chapter, we turn to put these individual issues into a much broader context, of informal social relationships, the institutional framework of schools, and specialist bereavement organisations. This then entails major issues for policy and professional practice.

Considering the social contexts of emotions raises issues about how we may view appropriate behaviour in public and private settings. The emotions of grief may be experienced by some individuals as disturbing, and highly disruptive of social situations, in ways that are very hard to anticipate and to manage. Adults may see this as a reason to avoid some social settings altogether until emotions can be brought under control. They may seek 'special' social contexts for dealing with such grief emotions, whether it be individual counselling, groups set up specifically for bereaved individuals, behind the closed door of a bedroom, or alone at a cemetery. But it may not be so easy for young people to draw their own boundaries, or withdraw from public settings, especially from schools. And yet, for young people generally, the teenage years may be a particular transitional time when they are expected to be learning to take responsibility for 'managing' their own emotions (Chapter 2). So how do young people deal with grief, both publicly and privately?

Loneliness and informal social relationships after bereavement

Popular conceptions of teenagers suggest that friends may become more important than families in the lives of young people. While this may underestimate the continuing significance of family relationships (Gillies, Ribbens McCarthy and Holland 2001), bereavement research does point to the key part played by peers. Some American research has shown that the presence of close friends can be experienced as extremely supportive and helpful by young people, and this is the category most often pointed to as being helpful (Gray 1989; Hogan and DeSantis 1994). Furthermore, close supportive relationships with peers may not be seen to carry the potential disadvantages (as discussed in Chapter 3, and see Gillies, Ribbens McCarthy and Holland 2001) that may be entailed in relationships with parents.

However, close supportive relationships with a few friends may occur alongside peer relationships that may be experienced as problematic, for example in terms of name calling, bullying and so on (Servaty and Hayslip 2001; Tyson-Rawson 1996; Worden 1996). 'They laugh at me and call me mumless'. 'My cousin hung himself and they keep telling me they can see things dangling from the trees' (callers to Childline, quoted in Cross 2002: 13–14). Less negatively, some writers (Monroe 1995; Wilby 1995) suggest that peers may be quite unsure about how to respond to bereavement, which points to general issues (discussed in Chapter 2) concerning the general privatisation of, and unfamiliarity with, death and bereavement in contemporary western societies.

Bereavement may thus also be associated with a more general withdrawal from peers. Studies in the USA have pointed to loneliness and a sense of being different as potential short- and long-term experiences for many young people bereaved of a parent or sibling (Davies 1991; Servaty and Hayslip 2001; Tyson-Rawson 1996; Worden 1996), and this resonates strongly with Neville's case study (Chapter 1).

In considering relationships beyond the immediate family, other adults may also constitute an important potential resource. Research on divorce points to the crucial part that can be played by strong relationships with another adult or friend (Amato 1993; Hetherington 2003), but there is very little empirical research concerning the implications of bereavement for a young person's relationships with wider kin (Hogan and DeSantis 1994).

In general terms, social support has been found to be associated with lower depression scores among parentally bereaved young people (Gray 1987), and this support may come from a number of different sources. Goodman (1986) found that parentally bereaved adolescents who were not in psychiatric treatment found support from the other parent, their peers and other individuals whose parent had died. But in her small-scale study of a school based sample of bereaved young people, Brown (2002) found that 57 per cent had not talked to anyone about their feelings. The main reasons were fear of upsetting other family members, not knowing where to go for help (this was in a locality where there were well-organised services available, linked to the school), and finding it too difficult or upsetting to talk. In another study, of young people bereaved of a peer, 76 per cent 'had been unable to share their feelings with *anyone* at the time of the loss and for a long time after' (Rosen 1984: 313, quoted by Ringler and Hayden 2000: 210, original emphasis). 'Mum died a year ago. I can't stop feeling sad. Dad just gets angry if I try to talk about it' (caller to ChildLine, quote in Cross 2002: 10). Isolation has also been identified as a major issue among young people who contact the Cruse internet site for young people (Salter and Stubbs 2004, discussed further below). And see also, below, debates about the value of talk.

The potential role for schools in addressing death and bereavement

Research concerning the significance of peers and other relationships beyond the immediate family points to the significance of schools as a major social context for the bereavement experiences of young people, and one estimate suggested that, at any given time, up to 70 per cent of schools are dealing with a bereaved child (Holland 1993). This, in turn, highlights issues of continuities and discontinuities around the bereavement experiences of young people. In what respects should bereavement be regarded as a majority experience, requiring general provisions for the education of all young people, and in what respects do some bereavements constitute a minority experience, that may require more specialised interventions than schools can provide?

Death and bereavement as part of the general curriculum

In the Introduction, we saw that significant bereavement is overwhelmingly the majority experience of young people, even in contemporary western societies. Furthermore, other evidence suggests that death and dying are things that the vast majority think about, suggesting that, 'children have a greater awareness of death than most adults would believe' (Bowie 2000: 24). And yet, as discussed in the Introduction, this is a topic that contemporary western societies have sidelined and rendered taboo.

Because school is where children spend a large proportion of their time, many see it as the obvious setting for both general information to be given, and for intervention to take place (Holland 1993; Rowling 2003; Sheras 2000; Wilby 1995). Some argue for its inclusion on mental health grounds (Rowling 2003), or grounds of spirituality (Higgins 1999), while others argue on the basis of the needs of the whole child (Stevenson 2000).

Generally, it is suggested, death education could dispel a lot of misinformation and myth. Consequently, when bereavement did occur, children would be better able to deal with it, whether it was a personal experience or something happening to a classmate. And, as we saw earlier, peer group reactions may be very significant, in both positive and negative ways. Schools can also normalise death and bereavement by teaching it across all areas of the curriculum, for example as part of English, science, history and geography, and even maths (Job and Frances 2004; Kenny 1998).

There are clear parallels here with debates about whether and how other topics should be dealt with in schools, such as sex or drugs education, within the context in the United Kingdom of Personal, Social and Health Education (PSHE). Death and bereavement are issues that need to be raised more generally within such broader debates.

There are thus some strong arguments made for the active inclusion of death and bereavement as topics in the general curriculum, and there are materials available for use in this area, sometimes with specialist help from voluntary sector services to back these up. But there is considerable doubt about whether or not it is in fact being included. Several authors suggest that one of the main difficulties may be the reluctance of staff to take on this area of the curriculum, partly because of their lack of specialist training (Carson and others 1995; Katz 2001; Papadatou and others 2002; Rowling 2003; Rowling and Holland 2000).

A growing number of initiatives are being created to help schools deal with death education and individual bereavement experiences. The UK government provides a framework for death and bereavement education within PSHE (see Box 4.1). This work has received recent endorsement by the UK House of Commons Select Committee on Health (2004), and the government response to this report (Secretary of State for Health 2004), which specifically supports the inclusion of death and bereavement as topics within PSHE, along with attendant training for teachers involved in this area. Nevertheless, the inclusion of death and bereavement in the general curriculum is not compulsory and many schools, because of the difficulties surrounding the subject, have tended not to address it. What provision there is, has tended to be random (Rolls and Payne 2003), although provisions and policies in other countries may show a marked difference from this UK picture (Rowling and Holland 2000). How far it will in practice be included within teacher training and PSHE remains to be determined.

Box 4.1: Resources for schools

Personal, Social and Health Education (PSHE) and Citizenship became part of the national curriculum requirement in English schools in August 2002. It is based on the 'planned provision for emotional and social development' of children (National Children's Bureau 2003), which Job and Frances argue 'would necessarily include discussion of the life and death continuum' (2004: 8).

Curriculum 2000, the national PSHE guidelines produced by the government, is a 26-page document detailing what should be taught as part of PSHE. The only mention of bereavement comes under Section 3 'Developing good relationships and respecting the differences between people'. It states that one of the things that children should be taught is: 'about the impact of separation, divorce and bereavement on families and how to adapt to changing circumstances'. Some resources are available, for example concerning the sudden death of a school pupil, from the Department for Education and Skills website (www.teachernet.gov.uk).

Various local education authorities produce their own information and guidance, in relation to curriculum development (for example Hertfordshire[1]) and school responses to death and sudden loss (for example Kent[2]).There is also a variety of other curriculum materials for use in this area, for example Machin (1993), Ward (1996). Most recently in the UK, the National Children's Bureau, in conjunction with the Childhood Bereavement Network, has provided an extensive discussion and guidelines in relation to bereavement issues in schools (Job and Frances 2004).

In some locations, specialist back-up and resources may be available to schools via local hospices and bereavement services (Rolls and Payne 2003). Winston's Wish operates in up to 300 schools and provides a 'grief support programme for children', as well as guidelines for schools in how to respond to a school related death.[3] Rainbows is a more broadly focused organisation which provides: 'training and programmes for children and adolescents who are grieving a death, separation, desertion, divorce or any other painful loss in their family' (www.rainbows.org, accessed June 2003). These programmes are run through schools, churches and other community services, and based on peer support groups.

Further resources and guidance are available from the websites of other voluntary bereavement organisations, including the Childhood Bereavement Trust (www.childbereavement.org.uk), Cruse Bereavement Care (www.crusebereavementcare.org.uk), and St Christopher's Candle Project (www.stchristophers.org.uk, based in London). Lowton (2004) provides general practical advice for school staff, along with a list of further publications.

Box 4.1: Resources for schools (cont'd)

Notes

1. See www.thegrid.org.uk/learning/pshe/bereavement.
2. Details are available from www.kented.org.uk/eps-web/teacher_death_and_loss.html.
3. Further details of their work can be found in Dowdney and others (1999), and at www.winstonswish.org.uk.

Management of emotions and emotional literacy

As well as pointing to common issues about how to teach other aspects of PSHE, such as sex or drugs education, the potentially disruptive emotions associated with bereavement and grief point to other general debates concerning the relevance and place of emotion management and emotional literacy in schools. Emotional literacy has been defined as: 'the ability to recognise, understand, handle, and *appropriately express* [their] emotions' (Sharp 2000: 8, emphasis added). At present, most school projects concerned with emotion and behaviour management are designed as a way of treating anti-social behavioural problems (Cohen 1999, 2001; Parke 1999; Sharp and Faupel 2002). In the UK, Sharp is a strong advocate for the incorporation of emotional literacy into the curriculum and schooling generally, and is associated with various initiatives run by Southampton Local Education Authority (for details see www.nelig.com/PDF/selig_guidelines.pdf).

Most existing projects, however, are based on changing the individual rather than looking at the social and organisational structures which may create such behaviour in the first place. The concept of teaching emotional literacy more broadly – including grief and bereavement – is a controversial one, particularly in the UK (Burman 2000; Carr 2000).

If emotional literacy is pursued in schools, it will need to be sensitive to cultural differences (whether related to gender, class, race, disability, etc.) with respect to what is considered to be the appropriate expression of emotions. It will also need to avoid therapeutic assumptions of the value of talk and emotional expression (discussed further later), and to take account of young people's own views of the desirability of keeping personal and private boundaries around their school lives (Alldred and others 2002; Edwards and Alldred 2000). Given these parameters, it may have a part to play in helping young people consider their own emotions – including grief – and those of their peers.

School based interventions for bereaved individuals

Although schools have always had to deal with individual pupils who have experienced a major bereavement, this has generally been on an ad hoc basis with no clear understanding of the effects of bereavement on children, and based on individual teachers' attitudes and experience rather than on any formal training (Eiser and others 1995). Over the last decade, however, the role of the school in helping children and young people deal with grief and bereavement has become a topic of debate and controversy (Katz 2001; Kenny 1998).

Holland (1993) argues that teachers themselves need help to understand what is happening psychologically and behaviourally to bereaved young people, and to have plans in place to deal with such situations both proactively and reactively. Teachers may also have to deal with children in their class who are terminally ill, or with the death of a class member (Bor and others 2002; Kenny 1998). But dealing with bereavement among their pupils can leave teachers 'emotionally drained' and with little sense of support that they are doing the right thing (Spall and Jordan 1999).

Given the ubiquity of bereavement experiences among young people (discussed in the Introduction) there may be a strong case for the inclusion of such issues as a core component of teacher training syllabi. However, short post-qualifying courses could also be useful for those already trained. Specialists could be available to contribute in specific circumstances, taking into account teachers' own feelings about dealing with such issues among their pupils. Others suggest that most teachers do have the relevant skills but need further knowledge and reassurance (Druce and Pentland 2004).

Among bereaved young people themselves there is a real range of views about how schools should deal with individual bereavement issues, and whether or not they want schools to be involved. Some children, especially adolescents, may not view school as an appropriate place to deal with emotions (Doka 2000; Ringler and Hayden 2000; Worden 1996), while others may want teachers actively to intervene. The overall message is that children's responses vary. While they need to be asked how they want it handled, often they are not consulted (Wood and Baulkwill 1995).

Crisis management

Rather different issues arise for schools in relation to traumatic incidents and accidents that occur within the school environment and to members of school communities. Such incidents have always happened (for example, the Aberfan disaster in Wales), but large-scale incidents in recent years, both within schools and society generally (such as 9/11, Hillsborough, Dunblane, Columbine High and so on), have heightened concerns about the need for schools to be prepared when a crisis occurs.

Most schools do not have a crisis management policy (Holland and Ludford 1995; Rowling 2003). But those schools that have had experience of such a crisis stress the usefulness of a pre-existing plan (Grant and Schakner 1993; O'Hara, Taylor and Simpson 1994; Sorensen 1989). While schools may not feel a need to develop their own individual plans, it may be important that they know where and how to access immediate guidelines in the unlikely event of actually experiencing such a disaster among their own pupils (O'Hara, Taylor and Simpson 1994; Shears 1995).

Specialist bereavement interventions by voluntary organisations in the UK

While schools and teachers may still be exploring how far, and in what ways, they should deal with bereavement issues within the education sector, specialist bereavement organisations in the voluntary sector have been developing their own services for children and young people, both in terms of providing support and advice to schools, and in terms of providing services directly to bereaved individuals outside the school setting (Rolls and Payne 2003). And, while this may arguably have initially happened 'with minimal national debate and no agreed standards or guidelines' (Stokes and others 1999: 291), May 2001 saw the advent in the UK of the Childhood Bereavement Network, enabling people to work towards increasing support for, and coordination of, services. The Network, operating within the auspices of the National Children's Bureau, has guidelines for best practice that cover such issues as safety, practice context, quality and accountability, and equality.[3]

Other recent UK developments have included various internet provisions. Cruse, the major national bereavement organisation, has set up an interactive website specifically for bereaved young people (*Crusenews*, Summer 2003), with opportunities for participants to exchange messages and to make their experiences and feelings known and available to others.[4] Winston's Wish, a major UK voluntary provider of services for bereaved children, offers specialist support through their website

3 Available from the Network Development Officer, Children's Bereavement Network, National Children's Bureau, 8 Wakley Street, London EC1V 7QE, tel: +44 (0)20 7843 6309, email: cbn@ncb.org.uk.

4 Available at www.rd4u.org.uk, or via the Cruse website, www.crusebereavementcare.org.uk, then click Youth Involvement Project.

(www.winstonswish.org.uk), with email support carrying the potential for both advantages and disadvantages compared with face-to-face work (Salter and Stubbs 2004).

The availability of face-to-face childhood bereavement services in the UK, however, is predominantly (86 per cent) based on geographical location (Rolls and Payne 2003), being completely absent in some localities and patchy in others. Of the 91 organisations identified by Rolls and Payne (2003) as providing services for children, 85 per cent were voluntary sector (although funding arrangements often included government money). Of the voluntary sector services, 41 were located in hospices and 75 per cent of bereavement services for children and young people could be regarded as specialist organisations in the sense that their remit was specifically focused on issues of bereavement and/or care of the dying. The remaining 25 per cent were part of other organisations, such as the NHS, or more general counselling services. Thirty-six per cent did not offer interventions with children or young people as individuals.

The availability of counselling and other bereavement support services for bereaved young people may thus be completely absent in some localities, and may be highly contingent in others. Even in those areas where a service is available, it may only be able to offer interventions with a very limited number of children, and may be available only to those where the death was anticipated.

How valuable is talk and counselling?

While voluntary organisations have been seeking to develop their services in response to what is seen as an urgent set of unmet needs, there is an ongoing (sometimes fierce) debate about how far counselling can appropriately ease the 'normal' distress of grief, and, more specifically, whether talking can help. Furthermore, the usefulness of talk generally may be significantly shaped by factors of class, culture and gender (Seale 1998).

There are deep controversies aroused by this debate. For example, in an article in *New Scientist* headlined, 'Counselling can add to trauma' (Coghlan 2002: 5), psychologist Simon Wessely of King's College London is quoted as saying: 'We have an ideology that it's "good to talk". But sometimes that's not so.' However, the article derives from an evaluation study by Wessley of a very specific service, which was a particular form of one-off bereavement counselling offered in the immediate aftermath of a disaster.

Some authors seem to imply that providing the opportunity to talk about feelings might actually create depressive symptoms that were not there before (Harrington and Harrison 1999). The query does arise, however, whether individuals who engage in talk may be more willing to describe depressive symptoms, and whether those referred to services may be more willing to 'admit' such symptoms. In a later study (Harrison and Harrington 2001) they found that the vast majority (88.5 per cent) of bereaved adolescents studied said they 'never or only rarely needed professional help for the way they were feeling about the deaths they had experienced'. The authors conclude that: 'there is little support, then, among adolescents themselves for the widespread development of specialized bereavement counselling services' (2001: 164).

However, discussing young people's support needs more generally, Hill (1999: 139) suggests that: 'the typical young person has little idea of the role of psychiatrists, psychologists or social workers, and for the most part no wish to consult them'. Research and practice with adolescents with general mental health difficulties confirm that this age group can be very 'hard-to-reach', with over 80 per cent of those in need failing to receive appropriate services (Griffiths 2004). Self-referrals are rare, with reliance instead on peers and sometimes family members, particularly mothers.

Young people may generally have a variety of strategies for dealing with problems, such as listening to music or being alone (Hill 1999), but for many, talking and listening may be one important outlet. A study specifically of young people bereaved of a peer found that hugs, talk and listening were all felt to be helpful, although often too limited in time (Ringler and Hayden 2000). Young people who have experienced a mental health crisis have also been found to value talk and listening (Leon and Smith 2001, cited by Griffiths 2004). Nevertheless, Worden found among bereaved children and young people that *not* talking about the deceased 'does not necessarily lead to more emotional and behavioural difficulties' (1996: 53).

Hill concludes:

> Many young people are suspicious of specialist professionals who are strangers to them. Children also want to be treated as whole human beings, not simply in relation to one 'problem' or 'disorder'.
>
> Among the implications for professionals are that effective direct work requires the opportunity to establish trust over time. In many circumstances, it may be more productive to work with the people in a child or young

> person's social network whom they already have confidence in.
> *(1999: 135)*

This may have particular relevance to bereavement counselling services provided by hospices to young people who experience sudden bereavement, rather than the anticipated death of someone already cared for by the hospice. The young person may be less receptive to such help than if it were offered in the context of the anticipated death of someone already cared for by the hospice

Services provided for bereaved young people recognise that talk and individual counselling is not always the most appropriate form of intervention for everyone. Other approaches may be offered instead, including play therapy (Webb 2000), ritual (Doka 2000), creative strategies (Fry 2000), or books (Corr 2000). As an alternative to individual help, interventions with families may offer an entirely different theoretical and practical approach (Grollman 2000; Kissane and Bloch 2002; McBride and Simms 2001; Sutcliffe and others 1998), though again, often centred on talk.

Talking with peers

Given young people's frequent reluctance to talk to adults, and need to establish trust in the context of unequal power relationships, and given the significance attached to support from friends discussed earlier, peer group interventions might seem to have much to offer to vulnerable young people (Cowie 1999). Tedeschi (1996) believes that group work with bereaved young people helps overcome isolation and helps to both 'contain' and 'express' emotions in a supportive setting.

In the USA, holiday camps may be provided for bereaved children (Sharp and Cowie 1998, based on Quarmby 1991), while in the UK, residential support groups are organised by some of the specialist bereavement services for children, such as Winston's Wish (discussed earlier). Providing opportunities for bereaved children and young people to talk to each other has been argued to help them considerably (Sharp and Cowie 1998; Wolfe and Senta 2002). However, it may be advantageous if those in the support groups have similar experiences of death – whether it be after a long illness, a sudden trauma or suicide (Johnson 1995), constituting another area where continuities and discontinuities of experiences may need to be sensitively considered. Currently in the UK, peer group support for bereaved young people is almost entirely based in specialist bereavement organisations, with 45 per cent of childhood bereavement services in Rolls and Payne's (2003) UK survey offering support groups.

Peer group support for bereaved children and young people could also be provided within schools (Silverman 2000). In the UK, schools can access support in setting up peer support services through the Peer Support Forum, which was founded by the Mental Health Foundation and ChildLine in 1998, and is currently part of NCB's Children's Development Unit (www.ncb.org.uk/psf/). The Forum encourages schools to facilitate students to offer help and support to fellow students. Projects remain under the direction and control of each individual school and can be implemented as listening services or as mentoring and befriending schemes (Sharp and Cowie 1998). The main issues that currently seem to be addressed by such schemes are those of bullying and racism, and a debate is needed about whether there is a case for also extending their role to cover family-related issues and bereavement more generally.

Implications for policy and practice

Major issues of policy and practice arise about how best to provide services to bereaved young people. Some of these may be particular to bereavement, while others may point to more general issues about how services and support may reach young people.

Organisation of services

While the provision of services by bereavement organisations based in the voluntary sector has been extremely important in extending support for bereaved children and young people and highlighting their needs, the present provisions are a long way from ensuring that help is readily available to all children and young people who might want it. However, we do not have the evidence to know the numbers of bereaved young people who have no access to such non-clinical services, or how great the demand for such support might be.

Apart from a lack of evidence about young people's own experiences and expressed need for support, there is still uncertainty among professionals about when it is appropriate to seek professional help. At which point should grief reactions be classed as 'pathological'? How should 'normal' grief be supported? These issues need to be addressed.

Furthermore, apart from controversies concerning the value of talk discussed earlier, there is also confusion at times about the nature and goals of different sorts of services and interventions. Stokes and others (1999) differentiate between statutory support services that are mental health based, and community based services that offer a more general level of information and support, with the two offering distinct but complementary services, each requiring different levels of skill and training: 'It is important to acknowledge that professional support or "therapy" may not be routinely appropriate for all bereaved children and young people. This does not mean, however, that no level of support can be offered at all' (Stokes and others 1999: 293). Community based services, they suggest, should be funded by monies specially raised in local communities, and provided in settings outside statutory mental health services, which may be less stigmatising (Meltzer and others 2000), although referrals would be made on to mental health services as necessary. Even a single phone call can provide important information and support (Levy 2004).

In the UK currently, statutory and voluntary services are likely to remain distinct, but there is a need for better working relationships between the statutory mental health and voluntary bereavement services, to enable cross-referral to take place effectively when needed and a better appreciation of what each has to offer.

Stokes and others argue that community based services should routinely be offered to all bereaved children and their families. However, issues remain about how such a universal service may be delivered and to whom. Their own discussion later clarifies that they are considering children bereaved of a sibling or parent, so omitting those bereaved of a peer. Furthermore, young people at risk of social exclusion may be the ones most likely to be without any access to services (Rolls and Payne 2003), and there may be particular issues about how to fund and provide services in particularly deprived areas. And yet these areas may be the ones where support is most needed by bereaved children, given that young people in such areas are more likely to experience significant bereavements in their lives (discussed in the Introduction) and to be living in localities where others' own resources to provide support have been depleted by a variety of stresses. In the light of the evidence, considered in Chapter 3, concerning the significance of existing vulnerabilities and of multiple losses and disadvantages for the risk of negative outcomes as a result of bereavement, this is a major issue for policy makers to address in conjunction with voluntary sector providers.

Referral processes

Besides such questions of the organisation and scope of services, there are also major concerns about how young people may be *referred* to any general or clinical support services. Dowdney and others (1999) suggest that GPs and primary health workers may have a particular role to play in referring young people to bereavement services. However, this was found not to be happening as much as it might, with a serious mismatch between need for, and provision of, services. This may result partly through lack of appropriate training (Lloyd-Williams 1999). In the context of sudden deaths particularly, Smith and Browne (2004) suggest that hospitals may also have an important part to play in ensuring that where no other support is in place affected children are identified and referred to a bereavement facilitator. A variety of general professionals could also act as sources of information after bereavement, including funeral directors and clergy.

In the family context, Gersten and others (1991) found that surviving mothers were much more likely than surviving fathers to seek help for their parentally bereaved children. It is also worth noting that, as Stuber and others (2002), found out in their study of post 9/11 trauma in Manhattan, it was the level of the parent's stress, rather than the child's, that related to children and young people being referred for counselling.

This points to the importance of facilitating young people's own direct access to support and services. As we saw with Neville's case study (Chapter 1) it is clear that bereaved family members do 'protect' each other from knowledge of each other's distress. Would Neville have taken up opportunities to talk (outside of the research interviews in which he was involved) if they had been available to him, and what format would have been appropriate for him? How could he have accessed them? Brown's (2002) small UK study is important in showing the extent to which bereaved young people may be unaware of services available to them, even in a locality where service provision is relatively well-organised and integrated with schools. This suggests the importance of provision of information to young people in ways that are easily accessible to them, as well as the provision of the services as such.

These issues of accessing support after bereavement parallel discussions about the provision of help services more broadly to young people (Griffiths 2004). Adolescents generally may have little awareness of services available, and find them hard to access when they do try to do so. Studies of those most likely to use services indicate that it is the more privileged, and those with supportive families, who are likely to access help (Tijhuis and others 1990, cited by Griffiths 2004) and to have positive expectations about the possibilities for change. This again returns us to questions about how to help bereaved young people in less advantaged circumstances, and also how to integrate information about bereavement into general services and information sources for young people, such as helplines.

Evaluating interventions

Evaluating different types of interventions is another much debated issue. Numerous publications provide qualitative accounts (often underpinned by strong beliefs) of the positive benefits for children and young people in being involved in some form of intervention programme after a major bereavement (for example Sharp and Cowie 1998; Wolfe and Senta 1995, 2002). There have also been numerous quantitative evaluation studies that have sought to assess the effectiveness of such interventions. However, there are serious methodological problems with the great majority of these studies. These include the ethics of controlling individuals' access to services for research purposes, the nature of the outcome being measured, and the enormous range of different sorts of interventions that may be offered (Curtis and Newman 2001; Schneiderman and others 1994; Schut and others 2002; Stokes, Wyver and Crossley 1997).

There is also a question mark over how to measure the effectiveness of an intervention. Should it be measured on the basis of participants' own views or by reference to measured outcomes (Small and Hockey 2001)? Some evidence also suggests that the effectiveness of therapeutic interventions generally varies according to the level of motivation of those taking part (Garfield 1994, cited by Schut and others 2002). This is in line with the discussion in Chapter 3, concerning the significance of individual meanings in mediating the impact of bereavement generally, but again, it increases the complexity of evaluating interventions.

Quantitative evaluation studies have generally focused on programmes offered to *all* children who have been significantly bereaved rather than programmes that specifically identify bereaved children considered to be at increased risk. Two relevant reviews (Curtis and Newman 2001; Schneiderman and others 1994) find the evidence to be too inconclusive to be able to recommend such interventions. Meanwhile, Harrington and Harrison (1999) suggest the possibility of active harm resulting from such interventions, although none of the evaluation studies we considered gave evidence of such harmful effects.

Others, however, interpret the evaluation studies more favourably for interventions for children and young people in particular, suggesting that there is more evidence that such children's programmes do help them cope with their loss than there is for adult intervention programmes (Schut and others 2002).

Peer support groups have been found to be valuable by both teachers and peer supporters (Cowie 1998; Cowie and others 2002), although this was specifically with respect to bullying. Peer support group interventions have also been evaluated as leading to improvements for primary school children whose parents were divorcing (Wilson and others 2003).

Overall, it is clear that more and better evaluation studies of different forms of bereavement intervention are needed. In addition to the need for methodological rigour, these need to cover a range of different sorts of interventions, referral processes and outcome measures, alongside 'an assessment of naturally occurring social support before, during and after the intervention takes place' (Schut and others 2002: 732).

There may also be arguments for a greater range of methodologies for studying outcomes, including qualitative techniques (Curtis and Newman 2001). There is scope, too, for broadening out from studies of bereavement interventions to consider what is to be learned from evaluations of other sorts of intervention programmes with young people.

Given the complexity of the issues to be addressed by rigorously quantitative evaluation studies of interventions with bereaved children and young people, it may be unrealistic to defer providing such services until there is a quantitative evidence base to underpin them.

Conclusions

There is research evidence of the importance – both positively and negatively – of peer relationships for bereaved young people, along with some suggestion of the possibility of loneliness as a (long-term) outcome of significant bereavement for some young people. It is also clear that many bereaved young people do not talk to anyone about their grief, although it is not apparent how many of these would like opportunities to talk, nor to whom.

While there would seem to be some forceful arguments for including 'death education' in the general schools curriculum, it seems likely that teachers generally feel ill-equipped to deal with it. It would therefore appear to be rarely implemented – although we have no research evidence to know for certain on this point. Its general inclusion in the curriculum would seem to have much to recommend it, both as a means of educating young people as individuals, and also as a means of equipping them to offer support to others when needed.

There are ongoing, fierce debates about whether or not help with grief is something that all bereaved young people may need or would benefit from and, if so, what might be the most appropriate setting for providing such help. There might, in the long run, be a risk of conveying a message to young people that a major crisis, such as a significant bereavement, is difficult to manage without organised support. Interventions thus need to build on young people's existing informal supports wherever possible. Peer support groups, whether in schools or provided by bereavement services, therefore appear to have particular advantages. At the same time, the general privatisation and medicalisation of death and bereavement may have disabled informal sources of support from being effective after bereavement; and several studies point to an absence of support or information from more general professionals, such as teachers, clergy and general medical personnel.

It is crucial to distinguish here between policies to make services *available and known* to all who might want them, and policies aimed at *providing* them as a matter of course for all bereaved children. Overall, a range of supports and interventions is likely to be needed, given the range of ways that individual young people cope with difficulties in their lives. They may also need to be available over a much longer time period than is generally the case at present.

Such interventions need to be much better coordinated across the range of service providers, including educational psychologists, teachers, primary health care workers, mental health professionals, youth workers and voluntary bereavement counselling services. We need an open debate about how best to achieve this. There is also a need for much more effective evaluation of interventions.

There are also key issues to be addressed about referral processes, which appear to be currently quite haphazard. It is likely that the young people most in need of bereavement support services may be the least likely to be referred to them – for example, vulnerable young people living in disadvantaged areas.

The literature review shows we know very little about many key aspects of how to help young people in ways that they will find appropriate and effective, given that the existing research is very largely based on people who are already in contact with services. We have very little evidence about how bereaved young people generally view their needs and how they may (or may not) cope in the absence of such services or interventions. We do not know how many more young people may be struggling to 'cope', like Neville, or facing increased vulnerability, like Brian, even years after a significant bereavement.

5. Conclusions

Our remit was to review and map the main areas of the literatures on bereavement and young people. Certain key features of these literatures stand out as prominent.

Bereavement as a general or specialised topic

The great majority of the literatures treat bereavement as a specialised topic. The empirical work focuses on bereavements that are seen to be 'significant' or 'traumatic' in terms of their potential implications for the individual's life experiences, particularly deaths of parents and siblings, while bereavement as a result of death of a peer has been largely neglected. Researchers have also sought to demarcate 'normal' from 'pathological' grief reactions as a way of targeting interventions.

Yet it is clear that experience of some form of major bereavement (of a close relative or friend) is the majority experience of young people. It could, therefore, be usefully regarded as a 'normal' feature of growing up. Not just specialist bereavement services, but mainstream services for young people need to be aware of bereavement issues too, and bereavement issues need to be mainstreamed.

We believe it is important to look at bereavement as both a source of difference (that is where it is a major, traumatic event) and of continuity (as part of life's rich tapestry) in young people's experiences. Our case studies (Chapter 1) exemplified this, but there is very little research that includes this range of bereavement experiences.

Understanding bereavement as a form of loss – or perhaps, more neutrally, as a source of change – alongside other types of loss or change in life, may help reduce the sense of difference because it may be seen as part of an ongoing pattern of experience. But not all bereavements are experienced as losses, while some bereavements may be so overwhelming they may seem quite unlike any other experience of loss or change.

Different research approaches

Our literature search revealed that the specific issue of bereavement and young people has largely been left unaddressed by sociologists, who have tended to leave this area to psychologists and the more individually focused professionals (Chapter 2). Psychology, counselling, therapeutic and medically based literatures have been strong on empirical evidence, and on theorising individual grief processes, but they are weaker on theorising at the broader level of the meanings of contemporary experiences of death and bereavement in cultural contexts, and researching the social processes in which individual bereavement experiences are set. They tend to seek universal statements about grief processes and reactions, and to neglect socially patterned differences within and between their research samples – although these might in themselves help to account for some of the contradictions between different research findings.

Much of the evidence is American based. We cannot just assume that it can be automatically translated into a UK context, where both institutions and cultures may be quite different – for example, with regard to religious affiliations or levels of violence. Much research is also based on very limited samples, and we need more research from young people who are not in contact with services.

We also believe the split between the contributions of psychological and sociological work to our understandings of bereavement in the lives of young people is unnecessary. There is a need for more integrated theoretical frameworks and interdisciplinary empirical work (Ribbens McCarthy 2006, forthcoming). Such models need to take account of a variety of individual, social and cultural dimensions, including the variable meanings that individuals may ascribe to particular events.

Are young people's needs in major bereavement different from those of other age groups?

Psychologists and clinicians have suggested that bereavement may be particularly complex and raise specific issues for individuals in their teenage years who are dealing with specific adolescent developmental tasks (Fleming and Balmer 1996; Raphael 1984; see also Chapter 2). Significant bereavements may also, in some circumstances, be experienced as a crisis of personal identity and biographical disruption that may carry implications into adulthood.

Yet bereavement needs to be understood in context. The institutionally based social status of 'youth' is one such context, carrying implications of relative powerlessness and ambiguity about expectations for self-responsibility and emotion management. If bereavement may be experienced as a major source of vulnerability and insecurity under some circumstances, this may be compounded for those who already feel a heightened sense of vulnerability and insecurity through being positioned as a 'young person'. Bereavement and youth are both characterised as transitions, and as potential sources of disruption, so their conjunction may potentially lead to a 'double jeopardy'.

Bereavement as a 'risk factor' in young people's lives

Research into bereavement as a 'risk' factor in young people's lives (Chapter 3) has focused on a (limited) range of different types of outcomes:

- risk for social disadvantage outcomes (e.g. educational qualifications, offending, employment)
- risk for personal outcomes (e.g. physical health and mental health).

Outcomes may be considered under quite different (long- and short-term) time trajectories. Long-term consequences, such as social isolation or difficulties in close relationships, may be harder to spot and may be overlooked by professionals working with young people. Ideas that people 'get over' bereavements may sometimes be misleading and unhelpful, even though the majority of bereaved young people may appear to 'cope' well, or at least adequately.

The research findings reached an open verdict on whether childhood/teenage loss of a parent through death is 'worse or better than divorce'. We suggest that it is not helpful to consider bereavement issues through this sort of question.

We considered a number of areas that have been researched and found, by at least some studies, to be issues that may be affected by significant bereavement (primarily researched in terms of the death of a parent). Such issues include:

- educational and employment status
- leaving home early

- early sexual and partnering activities
- criminal or disruptive behaviours
- depression, in the short and longer term
- self-concept and self-esteem.

Much of the evidence is, however, very complex and often contradictory. This may reflect differences and inadequacies in the methodologies used, particularly the nature of the samples studied; the possibility that bereavement may have opposite effects for different individuals, which are masked in large-scale statistical analyses; and the need to take into account the meaning that any bereavement has for the particular individual concerned.

Furthermore, in determining the level of risk, a number of cross-cutting factors come into play, even in relation to just one category (parental death). These include, for example: the gender of the young person and of the dead parent; social class; household resources; the history of the pre-bereavement relationship; whether or not the surviving parent remarries; the nature of the family environment after death; other supports available; aspects of personality; and the significance of other losses experienced.

This variety of factors may be understood via models that consider both resources and stressors at the level of:

- the individual
- family and social relationships
- broader structural issues such as class, material circumstances, race and gender.

These complex interwoven factors make risk assessment very difficult. Some factors, in particular material ones, can reduce the risk (for example not being forced to move home because of the death). For some young people, though, bereavement may be compounded by other disadvantages or multiple difficult life events, and this may clearly indicate an increased risk of negative outcomes. Furthermore, bereavement and multiple losses are much more likely to be experienced by young people who are already disadvantaged, but these young people are less likely to have organised support available to them.

Life experiences over time may enable some individuals to feel empowered to deal constructively and actively with the trauma of significant bereavement. For others, however, life experiences may successively disempower them, making life appear full of unpredictable and alarming uncertainties. It is not known whether bereavement itself increases the risk of subsequent adverse life experiences, but such experiences of multiple bereavements or compound disadvantages are likely to be unevenly distributed across localities, given the known link between premature death and inequalities related to social class and geography.

These difficulties in assessing risk mean that policies need to ensure that support services are available – over a long time – to *all* young people, since major bereavement does carry the potential for short- and long-term consequences, But policies *also* need to pay particular attention to the needs of bereaved young people in disadvantaged circumstances, and professionals need to be aware that bereavement may be a relevant issue in the life histories of particularly troubled and vulnerable young people.

A hotch-potch of provision and support

Friends are the single most often cited category of people who have been found to be helpful by bereaved young people, but peer relationships may well also add to the difficulties through contributing to a sense of difference or stigma, or outright bullying. High numbers of young people may speak to no one at all about even a major bereavement, and they may seek to 'protect' other family members from difficult feelings. Some family relationships may deteriorate sharply after bereavement, becoming conflictual or even abusive.

The qualitative evidence suggests that there are few social practices available to young people to make their grief visible. This is exacerbated by the failure of policies and services to understand bereavement as a majority experience for young people. Our research has highlighted concerns that loss and grief are seen as specialised matters, and therefore cut off from mainstream services. This is almost certainly compounded by wider cultural difficulties in dealing with bereavement, and the privatisation of grief in western societies.

The bereavement services currently provided for young people, whether through schools or bereavement organisations, are patchy and largely dependent on location. There are strong arguments for particular attention to be paid to bereavement support in those areas or localities where the need is likely to be highest, but current provisions are likely to be least available, namely areas of deprivation and disadvantage generally.

Existing bereavement services are also strongly focused on family bereavements, rather than bereavements of other types such as death of peers or partners. There is undoubtedly an important role to be played by specialist services, whether based in statutory mental health services or voluntary bereavement organisations. But there also needs to be much better integration and understanding of bereavement issues across the range of services that play a part in the lives of young people. There is also a need for cooperation and mutual insights and respect between different services.

Strong arguments can be made for including death and bereavement as part of the general school curriculum. There is provision for this within Personal, Social and Health Education (PSHE) and Citizenship, and relevant curriculum materials are available. However, many teachers may feel ill-equipped to handle this. Better training needs to be generally available to teachers in dealing with this issue, alongside the input of bereavement services within schools.

Finding ways of helping young people to talk about their experience – if they want such opportunities – is an important area for further work by researchers and practitioners. There is a need to recognise the wide range of ways in which young people may respond to bereavement and to work with their own preferred ways of dealing with stressful events. At the same time, it is clear that many bereaved young people do not get to talk to anyone about their feelings and experiences. This variability points to the need for a considerable range of interventions, in terms of intensity, duration, content and providers. Young people also vary a good deal in how far they want to be able to discuss bereavement experiences in educational settings, and it is important for teachers to establish the young person's own preferences. There is also a need to recognise and work with great variability around the bereavement experience itself, in terms of the category of loss, the cause of death, relevant social circumstances, and individual meanings and responses.

Peer support groups, either within or outside schools, are a promising way of enabling young people to support each other and perhaps reduce stigma. Much would depend, however, on whether or not such groups are able to build closely upon young people's own varied experiences and perceptions, rather than trying to impose an 'expert' model of what are considered to be appropriate grief reactions and processes.

Evaluating interventions for bereaved young people is a complex and difficult issue. Research suggests that interventions with children and young people may have more beneficial results than with older individuals. Interventions – from death education, to peer groups, to individual counselling – need to be evaluated in terms of whether they enhance or undermine individuals' own abilities and capacities to deal with future losses and crises.

It is also important to consider how young people can find out about any services that may be available (for example through funeral directors, hospital staff, GPs, Cruse, leaflets available in schools, general youth counselling and information services). Existing research has paid very little attention to the processes by which bereaved young people gain access, or referrals, to services. This issue needs to be considered also within the much broader context of general health education policies, and debates about how to provide information and support to disaffected or socially excluded young people, or to those already vulnerable, such as refugees.

Websites such as those provided by Cruse and Winston's Wish are very innovative and available to young people to use at their own discretion, but they are not widely known, and can only offer limited peer group support.

Implications for future research

Alongside theoretical issues and divisions that underpin different research traditions (discussed earlier), there are major omissions in our knowledge of how young people deal with issues of death and bereavement. Major gaps include:

- Firm base-line information about the prevalence of different forms of bereavement experience among young people.
- An understanding of bereavement as something experienced by the majority of young people – how do they experience and deal with such issues in their everyday lives and understandings; at what point does a particular bereavement become 'significant' and 'disruptive'?
- More complex and sophisticated quantitative research concerning assessment of 'risk' and 'resilience', based on more robust data sets and using advanced statistical analyses across a range of outcomes, both positively and negatively understood.
- Knowledge of the sorts of help and services such young people want, and how they can be helped to access them.
- Research into bereavement in relation to the death of a peer.
- The immediate social contexts of bereavement and the implications of bereavement for informal social relationships, including the risk of isolation and loneliness.
- A better understanding of the wider social contexts of bereavement, including socially patterned differences of a variety of types (ethnicity, class, regional, or based in particular neighbourhood or family histories).

- The impact of bereavement over a much longer time period. This might include more rigorous and direct attention to issues of bereavement within the national longitudinal and cohort studies of young people generally. It might also include narrative approaches using a retrospective as well as a contemporary perspective (for example Bradach and Jordan 1995; Eth and Pynoos 1994).

There are also key methodological issues that need to be addressed in future research:

- How to obtain widely based community based samples, and how to include those not in touch with any services, alongside adequate control groups.
- How to extend and integrate different methodological approaches – there has been a particular absence of ethnographic research that might help to understand bereavement in social context, and of narrative research that might help to provide both a longer time perspective and also insight into young people's own understandings and perspectives.

Implications for policy makers and practitioners

Issues of bereavement need to be integrated into mainstream services and policies for young people, and understood to be a majority experience, rather than being treated as a largely individualised (private) issue requiring specialist interventions. Its long-term implications also need to be recognised, both over an individual's childhood and teenage years, and also into adulthood.

This review has suggested the following issues need to be addressed:

- Although the current research is not conclusive and needs to be strengthened, parental bereavement may put an individual at greater risk of social exclusion and mental health difficulties.
- Bereavement may have particularly harmful implications for the lives of young people who are already vulnerable or living in disadvantaged circumstances, or who have experienced multiple problems. Some individuals seem to encounter particularly high levels of difficulties in their lives and these are strongly at risk of mental health and other problems (such as drug use, offending), and these are the young people least likely to have access to services. This may require some targeting of resources.
- A range of services and opportunities are needed for support, based on a variety of activities, from the provision of a single phone contact to individual or family

based interventions, to peer group support, to particular provisions for specific circumstances (for example bereavement through suicide). This range of services needs to be better integrated and coordinated so that all bereaved young people do have help potentially available if they want it, and so that they know how to access this.

- Death education needs to be much more widely and systematically included in schools, as a key aspect of general education for life, and as a way of equipping individuals to help both themselves and others through mutual support and understanding in relation to bereavement experiences.
- Young people's own views need to be respected and listened to, in relation both to their own bereavement experiences and the best ways in which to offer support and services.

People seek explanations and some sense of justice or morality in the face of human mortality and suffering. Young people particularly may struggle with such questions. The disruption of bereavement for young people may be a difficult issue that society generally has turned its face away from, but it is a topic requiring more direct attention from mainstream policies and services for young people.

Appendix: What we know from statistical data about the number of young people who experience bereavement

Experience of the death of a parent

Kiernan (1992), using data from the UK National Child Development Study, for children at age 16, found that 5.5 per cent had experienced family disruption through death of a parent.

Wadsworth (1979), using data from the UK National Survey of Health and Development, presents figures that seem to indicate 6.2 per cent had experienced the death of a parent at age 15.

In a later study (Wadsworth 1991), the figures seem to indicate 7.4 per cent overall at age 15, with 6.5 per cent among non-manual families, and 8.1 per cent among manual families.

By age 36, almost half of all people had lost at least one of their parents (Wadsworth 1991).

West and Farrington's (1973) survey of 10-year-old boys drawn from schools in Cambridgeshire, UK, showed 6.8 per cent had a parent who had died.

Sweeting and others (1998), using longitudinal data from the Scotland Twenty-07 Study in 1987, present figures showing 39 of 1009 respondents at age 15 who had experienced the death of a parent, that is 3.9 per cent.

Servaty and Hayslip (2001, citing Wessel 1983) quote figures of 5 per cent of American children experiencing parental death before age 16, though another study found that 11 per cent of junior and senior high school students had experienced the death of a parent before their senior year (Ewalt and Perkins 1979).

Gersten and others (1991) cite Kliman (1979) as providing a figure of 5 per cent of children experiencing parental death by age 15 in the USA.

Deaths among teenagers and children

We sought statistics on how many young people die, as we felt this might give an indication of the levels of bereavement among siblings, peers, friends and lovers.

There was a dramatic decline in childhood mortality rates in the UK during the twentieth century, particularly due to a decline in infant mortality (www.statistics.gov.uk/downloads/theme_social/social_focus_in_brief/children/Social_Focus_in_Brief_Children_2002.pdf; accessed 23 February 2004).

Childhood death rates have continued to decline in recent years (since 1991) (www.statistics.gov.uk/STATASBASE/expodata/files/2588007273lscv; accessed 23 February 2004), although projections to 2021 show this decline slowing down or stalling (www.statistics.gov.uk/STATSBASE/expodata/Spreadsheets/D34-8.xls; accessed 23 February 2004).

Table 1: Mortality rates for under 25-year-olds, UK 1991-94: rates per 10,000 population

	Males	Females
Under 1 year	74	58
1–4	4	3
5–14	2	1
15–19	6	3
20–24	8	3

(Taken from Charlton 1996: Table 3.4)

The most likely experience of bereavement that young people may encounter among other young people or children, is that of an infant sibling, followed by a male friend or sibling aged 15 to 24.

In the USA, mortality rates for 15- to 24-year-olds rose between 1960-80, with a sharp rise in violent deaths (murder and suicide) (Berman 1986, cited by Balk 1995). '15–24 year olds make up the only age group whose death rate has consistently increased since 1960 [in the USA]' (Balk 1995: 83). This is not the case for the UK where death rates among 15- to 24-year-old males have been quite level since 1945, with some slight decline again in the 1990s. The mortality rates for this age group, however, continue to be much higher than for 5- to 14-year-old males. Similarly the ratio of male deaths over female deaths is much greater for ages 15–24 than it is for ages 5–14. There has been no real improvement in the mortality rate for those aged around 18 in particular (Charlton 1996).

Experience of bereavement overall among young people

Harrison and Harrington (2001) provide perhaps the most comprehensive figures in the UK context, in relation to *bereavement generally* as a feature of teenagers' experiences. Their study was based on a convenience sample of two large secondary schools in Northern England. Subjects' ages ranged from 11–16. Of those on the school rolls, 86 per cent (1746) completed questionnaires. Almost 91 per cent were white.

4.1 per cent had lost a parent. Overall, the risk of parental death by age 16 was calculated to be about 6 per cent and risk of the death of a sibling was about 5 per cent (including stillbirths).

92.4 per cent reported having been bereaved of a first degree relative, second degree relative, other significant friend, relative or pet.

Brown (2002) reported that 82 per cent of her survey of 28 young people aged 15–16 in one school class in Northern England, reported an experience of bereavement where someone close had died, including grandparents, close friends, aunts, uncles, cousins.

Meltzer and others (2000) in a survey of mental health of 5–15-year-olds living in private households in the UK, found that 3 per cent of children had experienced the death of a parent or sibling, 6 per cent had experienced the death of a close friend, and 13 per cent the death of a grandparent. These figures may be expected to rise by the time all these children reach age 16.

In the USA, Ewalt and Perkins (1979) asked junior and senior high school students in two schools in Kansas (of different social mixes) about their experiences of bereavement. They found that nearly 90 per cent reported seeing a dead person and had lost a grandparent, aunt, uncle, sibling or someone else they cared about. Approximately 40 per cent had experienced the death of a close friend their own age.

References

Abrams, R (1992) *When Parents Die*. London: Charles Letts.

Agid, O and others (1999) 'Environment and vulnerability to major psychiatric illness: a case control study of early parental loss in major depression, bipolar disorder and schizophrenia', *Molecular Psychiatry*, 4, 2, 163–72.

Alldred, P and others (2002) *Minding the Gap: Children and Young People Negotiating Relations between Home and School*. London: Routledge Falmer.

Allen, C, Sprigings, N and Kyng, E (2003) *Street Crime and Drug Misuse in Greater Manchester*. Salford: University of Salford/Home Office.

Amato, PR (1993) 'Children's adjustment to divorce: theories, hypotheses and empirical support', *Journal of Marriage and the Family*, 58, 1, 23–28.

Amato, P (2000) 'The consequences of divorce for adults and children', *Journal of Marriage and the Family*, 62, 4, 1269–87.

Amaya, JFS (2002) 'How young people live and die in a violent country: the Columbian Case', Paper presented at the Conference of the European Sociological Association, Helsinki.

Anderson, M (1985) 'The emergence of the modern life cycle', *Social History*, 10, 1, 69–87.

Anderson, M 'The social implications of demographic change', in Thompson, FML (ed) (1990) *The Cambridge Social History of Britain 1750–1950 Volume 2: The People and Their Environment*. Cambridge: Cambridge University Press.

Aries, P (1974) *Western Attitudes to Death*. London: Marion Boyars.

Aries, P (1981) *The Hour of Our Death*. London: Allen Lane.

Balk, DE (1991) 'Death and adolescent bereavement: current research and future directions', *Journal of Adolescent Research*, 6, 1, 7–27.

Balk, DE (1995) *A Review of Adolescent Development: Early Through Late Adolescence*. Pacific Grove, CA: Brookes/Cole.

Balk, DE 'Adolescents, grief and loss', in Doka, KJ (ed) (2000) *Living with Grief: Adolescents and Loss*. Washington, DC: Hospice Foundation of America.

Balk, DE and Corr, CA 'Adolescents, developmental tasks and encounters with death and bereavement', in Corr, CA and Balk, DE (eds) (1996) *Handbook of Adolescent Death and Bereavement.* New York: Springer.

Balmer, LE (1992) *Adolescent Sibling Bereavement: Mediating Effects of Family Environment and Personality.* Toronto: York University Press.

Barry, M (2001) *Challenging Transitions: Young People's Views and Experiences of Growing Up.* London: Save the Children/Joseph Rowntree Foundation.

Beratis, S 'Suicidal attempts and suicides in Greek Adolescents', in Papadatou, D and Papadatos, C (eds) (1991) *Children and Death.* New York: Hemisphere.

Birtchnell, J (1972) 'Early parental death and psychiatric diagnosis', *Social Psychiatry*, 7, 202–10.

Black, D (1978) 'Annotation: the bereaved child', *Journal of Child Psychology and Psychiatry*, 19, 3, 287–92.

Black, D 'Family intervention with families bereaved or about to be bereaved', in Papadatou, D and Papadatos, C (eds) (1991) *Children and Death.* New York: Hemisphere.

Black, D (1993a) *Highlight. Children and Bereavement* (1). London: National Children's Bureau.

Black, D (2002) 'The family and childhood bereavement: an overview', *Bereavement Care*, 21, 2, 24–26.

Bode, J (1993) *Death is Hard to Live With: Teenagers Talk about How they Cope with Loss.* New York: Bantam Doubleday.

Bor, R and others (2002) *Counselling in Schools.* London: Sage.

Boswell, GR (1996) 'The needs of children who commit serious offences', *Health & Social Care in the Community*, 4, 1, 21–29.

Bowie, L (2000) 'Is there a place for death education in the primary curriculum?', *Pastoral Care*, 18, 22–27.

Bradach, K and Jordan, JR (1995) 'Long-term effects of a family history of traumatic death on adolescent individuation', *Death Studies*, 19, 4, 315–36.

Brannen, J and others (1994) *Young People, Health and Family Life.* Buckingham: Open University Press.

Brannen, J and others (2002) *Young Europeans, Work and Family: Futures in Transition.* London: Routledge, Taylor and Francis.

Brent, DA and others (1993) 'Psychiatric impact of the loss of an adolescent sibling to suicide', *Journal of Affective Disorders*, 28, 4, 249–56.

Brown, J (2002) *Young People and Bereavement Counselling: What Influences Young People in their Decision to Access Bereavement Counselling After the Death of Someone Close.* Unpublished Masters Dissertation. College of York St John. Leeds, University of Leeds.

Buchanan, A and Brinke, JT (1997) *What Happened when They Were Grown Up?* York: Joseph Rowntree Foundation.

Burman, E (2000) 'Emotions in the classroom and the institutional politics of knowledge', *Psychoanalytic Studies*, 3, 3–4, 313–24.

Bynner, J (2001) 'Childhood risks and protective factors in social exclusion', *Children and Society*, 15, 5, 285–301.

Canetti, L and others (2000) 'The impact of parental death versus separation from parents on the mental health of Israeli adolescents', *Comprehensive Psychiatry*, 41, 5, 360–68.

Carr, D (2000) 'Emotional intelligence, PSE and self-esteem: a cautionary note', *Pastoral Care*, 18, 3, 27–33.

Carson, JF and others (1995) 'An investigation of the grief counseling-services available in the middle schools and high-schools in the state of Mississippi', *Omega – Journal of Death and Dying*, 30, 3, 191–204.

Charlton, J 'Trends in all-cause mortality: 1841–1994', in Charlton, J and Murphy, M (eds) (1996) *The Health of Adult Britain, 1941–1994, Volume 1*. London: The Stationery Office.

Clark, DC, Pynoos, RS and Goebel, AE 'Mechanisms and process of adolescent bereavement', in Robert J. Haggerty, RJ and others (eds) (1994) *Stress, Risk and Resilience in Children and Adolescents: Processes, Mechanisms and Interventions*. Cambridge: Cambridge University Press.

Coghlan, A (2002) 'Counselling can add to post-disaster trauma', *New Scientist*, 26 June, 5.

Cohen, J (1999) *Educating Minds and Hearts: Social Emotional Learning and the Passage into Adolescence*. New York: Teachers College Press.

Cohen, J (2001) *Caring Classrooms/Intelligent Schools: The Social and Emotional Education of Young Children*. New York: Teachers College Press.

Corr, CA (1996) 'What do we know about grieving children and adolescents?', in Doka, KJ (ed) *Living with Grief: Children, Adolescents and Loss*. Washington, DC: Hospice Foundation of America.

Corr, CA (2000) 'Using books to help children and adolescents cope with death: guidelines and bibliography', in Doka, KJ (ed) *Living with Grief: Children, Adolescents and Loss*. Washington, DC: Hospice Foundation of America.

Cowie, H (1998) 'Perspectives of teachers and pupils on the experience of peer group support against bullying', *Educational Research and Evaluation*, 4, 2, 108–25

Cowie, H (1999) 'Editorial: peers helping peers: interventions, initiatives and insights', *Journal of Adolescence*, 22, 4, 433–36.

Cowie, H and others (2002) 'Knowledge, use of and attitudes towards peer support: a 2-year follow-up to the Prince's Trust survey', *Journal of Adolescence*, 25, 5, 453–67.

Cross, S (2002) *'I can't stop feeling sad': Calls to Childline about Bereavement*. London: Childline.

Curtis, K and Newman, T (2001) 'Do community-based support services benefit bereaved children? A review of empirical evidence', *Child Care Health and Development*, 27, 6, 487–95.

Davies, B 'Responses of children to the death of a sibling', in Papadatou, D and Papadatos, C (eds) (1991) *Children and Death*. New York: Hemisphere.

Demi, AS and Gilbert, CM (1987) 'Relationship of parental grief to sibling grief', *Arch Psychiatric Nursing*, 1, 6, 385–91.

Desai, S and Bevan, D (2002) 'Race and Culture', in Thompson, N (2002) *Loss and Grief: A Guide to Human Services Practitioners.* Basingstoke: Palgrave.

Doka, KJ (2000) *Living with Grief: Children, Adolescents, and Loss.* Washington, DC: Hospice Foundation of America.

Douglas, JWB (1970) 'Broken families and child behaviour', *Journal of the Royal College of Physicians*, 4, 3, 203–10.

Douglas, JWB and others (1968) *All Our Future.* London: Peter Davies.

Dowdney, L (2000) 'Annotation: childhood bereavement following parental death', *Journal of Child Psychology and Psychiatry and Allied Disciplines*, 41, 7, 819–30.

Dowdney, L and others (1999) 'Psychological disturbance and service provision in parentally bereaved children: prospective case-control study', *British Medical Journal*, 319, 7206, 354–57.

Druce, C and Pentland, C (2004) 'Feeling Alone ... In School', Paper presented at the Childhood Bereavement Network Conference, *Feeling Alone, Feeling Different*, London.

Edwards, R and Alldred, P (2000) 'A typology of parental involvement in education centring on children and young people: negotiating familialisation, institutionalisation and individualisation', *British Journal of Sociology of Education*, 21, 3, 435–55.

Eisenbruch, M (1991) 'From post-traumatic stress disorder to cultural bereavement: diagnosis of Southeast Asian refugees', *Social Sciences and Medicine*, 33, 6, 673–80.

Eiser, C and others (1995) 'The place of bereavement and loss in the curriculum: teachers' attitudes', *Pastoral Care*, 13, 4, 32–37.

Elias, N (1985) *The Loneliness of the Dying.* Oxford, Blackwell.

Elliott, J and others (1993) *The Consequences of Divorce for the Health and Well-Being of Adults and Children.* Cambridge: University of Cambridge, Centre for Family Research.

Elliott, JL (1999) 'The death of a parent in childhood: a family account', *Illness, Crisis, Loss*, 7, 4, 360–75.

Eth, S and Pynoos, RS (1994) 'Children who witness the homicide of a parent', *Psychiatry – Interpersonal and Biological Processes*, 57, 4, 287–306.

Ewalt, P and Perkins, L (1979) 'The real experiences of death among adolescents: an empirical study', *Social Casework: The Journal of Contemporary Social Work*, 60, 9, 547–51.

Farrington, DP (1996) *Understanding and Preventing Youth Crime: Social Policy Research 93.* York: Joseph Rowntree Foundation.

Featherstone, M (1995) *The Body: Social Processes and Cultural Theory.* London: Sage.

Field, D (1996) 'Awareness and modern dying', *Mortality*, 1, 3, 255–66.

Finlay, IG and Jones, NK (2000) 'Unresolved grief in young offenders in prison', *British Journal of General Practice*, 50, 456, 569–70.

Fleming, S and Balmer, L 'Bereavement in adolescence', in Corr, CA and Balk, DE (eds) (1996) *Handbook of Adolescent Death and Bereavement.* New York: Springer.

Fleming, SJ and Adolph, R 'Helping bereaved adolescents: needs and responses', in Corr, CA and McNeil, JN (eds) (1986) *Adolescence and Death.* New York: Springer.

Fry, VL 'Part of me died too: creative strategies for grieving children and adolescents', in Doka, KJ (ed) (2000) *Living with Grief: Children, Adolescents and Loss.* Washington, DC: Hospice Foundation of America.

Furlong, A and Cartmel, F (1997) *Young People and Social Change: Individualization and Risk in Later Modernity.* Buckingham: Open University Press.

Gersten, JC and others (1991) 'Epidemiology and preventive interventions: parental death in childhood as an example', *American Journal of Community Psychiatry*, 19, 4, 481–98.

Giddens, A (1990) *The Consequences of Modernity.* Cambridge: Polity Press.

Giddens, A (1991) *Modernity and Self-Identity: Self and Society in the Late Modern Age.* Cambridge: Polity Press.

Gillies, V (2000) 'Young people and family life: analysing and comparing disciplinary discourses', *Journal of Youth Studies*, 3, 2, 211–28.

Gillies, V, Ribbens McCarthy, J and Holland, J (2001) *'Pulling Together, Pulling Apart': The Family Lives of Young People Aged 16-18.* York: Joseph Rowntree Foundation/Family Policy Studies Centre.

Goodman, RA (1986) 'Adolescent Grief Characteristics When a Parent Dies', unpublished PhD thesis, University of Colorado.

Goodyer, IM 'Life events and difficulties: their nature and effects', in Goodyer, IM (ed) (1995) *The Depressed Child and Adolescent: Developmental and Clinical Perspectives.* Cambridge: Cambridge University Press.

Gorer, G (1987) *Death, Grief and Mourning in Contemporary Britain.* London: Cresset Press.

Grant, L and Schakner, B (1993) 'Coping with the ultimate tragedy – the death of a student', *NASSP Bulletin.*

Gray, RE (1987) 'Adolescent response to the death of a parent', *Journal of Youth and Adolescence*, 16, 511–25.

Gray, RE (1989) 'Adolescents' perceptions of social support after the death of a parent', *Journal of Psychosocial Oncology*, 7, 3, 127–44.

Green, J (1991) *Death with Dignity: Meeting the Spiritual Needs of Patients in a Multi-Cultural Society, Books 1 and 2.* London: Nursing Times/MacMillan Magazines.

Griffiths, M (2003) 'Terms of engagement – reaching hard to reach adolescents', *Young Minds Magazine*, 62, Jan/Feb, http://www.youngminds.org.uk/magazine/62/griffiths.php (Accessed 7 February 2005).

Grollman, EA 'To everything there is a season: empowering families and natural support systems', in Doka, KJ (ed) (2000) *Living with Grief: Children, Adolescents, and Loss.* Washington, DC: Hospice Foundation of America.

Guerriero, AM and Fleming, SJ (1985) 'Adolescent bereavement: a longitudinal study', paper presented at the Annual Meeting of the Canadian Psychological Association, Halifax, Nova Scotia.

Haggerty, RJ (1994) *Stress, Risk and Resilience in Children and Adolescents: Processes, Mechanisms and Interventions.* Cambridge: Cambridge University Press.

Harrington, R and Harrison, L (1999) 'Unproven assumptions about the impact of bereavement on children', *Journal of the Royal Society of Medicine*, 92, 5, 230–33.

Harrington, R and Vostanis, P (1995) 'Longitudinal perspectives and affective disorder in children and adolescents', in Goodyer, IM (ed) (1995) *The Depressed Child and Adolescent: Developmental and Clinical Perspectives.* Cambridge: Cambridge University Press.

Harrison, L and Harrington, R (2001) 'Adolescents' bereavement experiences. Prevalence, association with depressive symptoms, and use of services', *Journal of Adolescence*, 24, 2, 159–69.

Hetherington, EM (2003) 'Social support and the adjustment of children in divorced and remarried families', *Childhood: A Global Journal of Child Research*, 10, 2, 217–53.

Higgins, S (1999) 'Death Education in the Primary School', *International Journal of Children's Spirituality*, 4, 1, 77–94.

Hill, M (1999) 'What's the problem? Who can help? The perspectives of children and young people on their well-being and on helping professionals', *Journal of Social Work Practice*, 13, 2, 135–45.

Hockey, J (1990) *Experiences of Death: An Anthropological Account.* Edinburgh: Edinburgh University Press.

Hockey, J (1996) 'Encountering the reality of death through professional discourses: the matter of materiality', *Mortality* 1, 1, 61–82.

Hogan, N and DeSantis, L (1994) 'Things that help and hinder adolescent sibling bereavement', *Western Journal of Nursing Research* 16, 2, 132–53.

Holland, Janet (2002) Personal communication, http://www.sbu.ac.uk/fhss/staff/janetholland.shtml.

Holland, John (1993) 'Child bereavement in Humberside primary schools: short report', *Educational Research*, 35, 3, 289–97.

Holland, John (2001) *Understanding Children's Experiences of Parental Bereavement.* London: Jessica Kingsley.

Holland, John and Ludford, C (1995) 'The effects of bereavement on children in Humberside secondary schools', *British Journal of Special Education*, 22, 2, 56–59.

House of Commons Health Committee, *Palliative Care*, Fourth Report of Session 2003–4, Volume 1. London: Stationery Office. http://www.parliament.the-stationery-office.co.uk/pa/cm200304/cmselect/cmhealth/454/454.pdf (Accessed 6 December 2004).

Iacovou, M and Berthoud, R (2001) *Young People's Lives: A Map of Europe.* Colchester: Institute for Social and Economic Research, University of Essex.

James, A, Jenks, C and Prout, A (eds) (1998) *Theorizing Childhood.* Cambridge: Polity Press.

Job, N and Frances, G (2004) *Childhood Bereavement: Developing the Curriculum and Pastoral Support.* London: National Children's Bureau.

Johnson, C 'Adolescent grief support groups', in Adams, DW and Deveau, EJ (eds) (1995) *Beyond the Innocence of Childhood Volume 3: Helping Children and Adolescents Cope with Death and Bereavement.* New York: Baywood.

Johnston, L and others (2000) *Snakes and Ladders: Young People, Transitions and Social Exclusion.* Bristol: Joseph Rowntree Foundation/Policy Press.

Jones, G and Wallace, C (1992)*Youth, Family and Citizenship.* Buckingham: Open University Press.

Katz, J (2001) *Grief, Mourning and Death Ritual.* Buckingham: Open University Press.

Kelly, J (2003) 'Changing perspectives on children's adjustment following divorce: a view from the United States', *Childhood: A Global Journal of Child Research,* 10, 3, 237–54.

Kendler, KS and others (1992) 'Childhood parental loss and adult psychopathology in women', *Archives of General Psychiatry,* 49, 2, 109–16.

Kenny, C (1998) *A Thanatology of the Child: Children and Young People's Perceptions, Experiences and Understandings of Life, Death and Bereavement.* Dinton: Quay Books.

Kiernan, KE (1992) 'The impact of family disruption in childhood and transitions made in young adult life', *Population Studies,* 46, 2, 213–34.

Kissane, DW and Bloch, S (2002) *Family Focused Grief Therapy: A Model of Family-Centred Care during Palliative Care and Bereavement.* Buckingham: Open University Press.

Krementz, J (1983) *How It Feels When a Parent Dies.* London: Victor Gollancz.

Langford, W and others (2001) *Family Understandings: Closeness, Authority and Independence in Families with Teenagers.* London: Joseph Rowntree Foundation/Family Policy Studies Centre.

Levete, S (1998) *When People Die.* UK: Copper Beech Books.

Levy, JM (2004) 'Unseen support for bereaved families', *Bereavement Care,* 23, 2, 25–26.

Liddle, M and Solanki, A (2002) *Persistent Young Offenders: Research on Individual Backgrounds and Life Experiences.* London: National Association for the Care and Resettlement of Offenders.

Lloyd-Williams, M (1999) 'Rapid response', *British Medical Journal,* 24 September, http://bmj.com/cgi/eletters/319/7206/354 (Accessed 16 January 2003).

Loeber, R and Dishion, T (1983) 'Early predictors of male delinquency: a review', *Psychological Bulletin,* 94, 1, 68–99.

Lowton, K (2004) *Supporting Bereaved Students in Primary and Secondary Schools,* London: King's College, London and the National Council for Hospice and Specialist Palliative Care Services.

Lowton, K and Higginson, IJ (2002) *Early Bereavement: What Factors Influence Children's Responses to Death?* London: King's College, London and the National Council for Hospice and Specialist Palliative Care Services.

Luthar, SS, Cicchetti, D and Becker, B (2000) 'The construct of resilience: a critical evaluation and guidelines for future work', *Child Development,* 71, 3, 543–62.

Machin, L (1993) *Working with Young People in Loss Situations.* Harlow: Longman.

Mack, KY (2001) 'Childhood family disruptions and adult well-being: the differential effects of divorce and parental death', *Death Studies*, 25, 5, 419–43.

Maclean, M and Kuh, D 'The long-term effects for girls of parental divorce', in Maclean, M and Groves, D (eds) (1991) *Women's Issues in Social Policy*. London: Routledge.

Maclean, M and Wadsworth, MEJ (1988) 'The interests of children after parental divorce: a long-term perspective', *International Journal of Law and the Family*, 2, 155–66.

Mayall, B (2002) *Towards a Sociology for Childhood: Thinking from Children's Lives*. Buckingham: Open University Press.

McBride, J and Simms, S (2001) 'Death in the family: adapting a family systems framework to the grief process', *American Journal of Family Therapy*, 29, 1, 59–73.

McCord, J 'A longitudinal view of the relationship between paternal absence and crime', in Gunn, J and Farrington, DP (eds) (1982) *Abnormal Offenders, Delinquency and the Criminal Justice System*. Chichester: John Wiley and Sons.

Mellor, P (1993) *The Sociology of Death*. Oxford: Blackwell.

Meltzer, H and others (2000) *The Mental Health of Children and Adolescents in Great Britain: The Report of a Survey carried out in 1999 by Social Survey Division of the Office for National Statistics on behalf of the Department of Health, the Scottish Health Executive and the National Assembly for Wales*. London: The Stationery Office.

Monroe, B 'It is impossible *not* to communicate – helping the bereaved family', in Smith, SC and Pennells, M (eds) (1995) *Interventions with Bereaved Children*. London: Jessica Kingsley.

Morin, SM and Welsh, LA (1996) 'Adolescents' perceptions and experiences of death and grieving', *Adolescence*, 31, 123, 585–95.

Morrow, V (1998) *Understanding Families: Children's Perspectives*. London: National Children's Bureau.

National Children's Bureau (2003) *Factsheet on PSHE/Citizenship Education*. London: National Children's Bureau.

Neuberger, J (1987) *Caring for Dying People of Different Faiths*. London: Austen Cornish.

O'Hara, DM, Taylor, R and Simpson, K (1994) 'Critical incident stress debriefing: bereavement support in schools – developing a role for an LEA Educational Psychology Service', *Educational Psychology in Practice*, 10, 1, 27–33.

Papadatou, D and others (2002) 'Supporting the bereaved child: teachers' perceptions and experiences in Greece', *Mortality*, 7, 3, 324–39.

Parke, J (1999) 'Emotional literacy: education for meaning', *International Journal of Children's Spirtuality*, 4, 1, 19–28.

Parkes, C (1998) *Bereavement*. Harmondsworth: Penguin.

Parkes, CM and others (1997) *Death and Bereavement across Cultures*. London: Routledge.

Perschy, MK (1997) *Helping Teens Work Through Grief*. Washington, DC: Accelerated Development.

Quarmby, D (1991) 'Peer counselling with bereaved adolescents', *British Journal of Guidance and Counselling*, 21, 2, 196–211.

Raphael, B (1984) *The Anatomy of Bereavement: A Handbook for the Caring Professionals.* London: Unwin Hyman.

Ribbens McCarthy, J (2006) *Young People's Experiences of Bereavement: Towards an Interdisciplinary Approach.* Buckingham: Open University Press (forthcoming).

Ribbens McCarthy, J and Edwards, R (2000) 'Moral tales of the child and the adult: narratives of contemporary family lives under changing circumstances', *Sociology*, 34, 4, 785–804.

Riches, G and Dawson, P (2000) *An Intimate Loneliness: Supporting Bereaved Parents and Siblings.* Buckingham: Open University Press.

Ringler, LL and Hayden, DC (2000) 'Adolescent bereavement and social support: peer loss compared to other losses', *Journal of Adolescent Research*, 15, 2, 209–30.

Rodgers, B (1990) 'Adult affective disorder and early environment', *British Journal of Psychiatry*, 157, 4, 539–50.

Rodgers, B and Pryor, J (1998) *Divorce and Separation: The Outcomes for Children.* York: Joseph Rowntree Foundation.

Rolls, L and Payne, S (2003) 'Childhood bereavement services: a survey of UK provision', *Palliative Medicine*, 17, 5, 423–32.

Rowling, L (2003) *Grief in School Communities: Effective Support Strategies.* Buckingham: Open University Press.

Rowling, L and Holland, J (2000) 'Grief and school communities: the impact of social context, a comparison between Australia and England', *Death Studies*, 24, 1, 35–50.

Rutter, M (1999) 'Resilience concepts and findings: implications for family therapy', *Journal of Family Therapy*, 21, 2, 119–44.

Rutter, M (2000) 'Psychosocial influences: critiques, findings and research needs', *Development and Psychopathology*, 12, 3, 375–405.

Rutter, M and others (1998) *Anti-Social Behaviour by Young People.* Cambridge: Cambridge University Press.

Saler, L and Skolnick, N (1992) 'Childhood parental death and depression in adulthood – roles of surviving parent and family environment', *American Journal of Orthopsychiatry*, 62, 4, 504–16.

Salter, A and Stubbs, D (2004) 'Feeling Alone ... Getting Help From the Internet', paper presented at the Childhood Bereavement Network Conference, *Feeling Alone, Feeling Different*, London.

Scheper-Hughes, N (1992) *Death Without Weeping: The Violence of Everyday Life in Brazil.* Berkeley: University of California Press.

Scheper-Hughes, N and Sargent, C (1998) *Small Wars: The Cultural Politics of Childhood.* Berkeley: University of California Press.

Schneiderman, G and others (1994) 'Do child and parent bereavement programs work?', *Canadian Journal of Psychiatry*, 39, 4, 215–17.

Schoon, I and Montgomery, SM (1997) 'The relationship between early life experiences and adult depression', *Zeitschrift Fur Pscyhosomatiische Medizin Und Psychoanalyse*, 43, 4, 319–33.

Schoon, I and Parsons, S (2002) 'Competence in the face of adversity: the impact of early family environment and long-term consequences', *Children and Society* 16, 4, 260–72.

Schut, H and others 'The efficacy of bereavement interventions: determining who benefits', in Stroebe, M, Stroebe, W and Hasson, RO (eds) (2002) *Handbook of Bereavement: Theory, Research and Interventions*. New York: Cambridge University Press.

Seale, C (1998) *Constructing Death: The Sociology of Dying and Bereavement*. Cambridge: Cambridge University Press.

Secretary of State for Health (2004) *Government Response to House of Commons Committee Report on Palliative Care Fourth Report of Session 2003–4*. London: HMSO
http://www.dh.gov.uk/PublicationsAndStatistics/Publications/PulbicationsPolicyAndGuidanceArticle/fs/en?CONTENT_ID=4089264&chk=GVBNjV (Accessed 6 December 2004).

Seiffge-Krenke, I (2000) 'Causal links between stressful events, coping style and adolescent symptomology', *Journal of Adolescence*, 23, 6, 675–91.

Servaty, HL and Hayslip, B (2001) 'Adjustment to loss among adolescents', *Omega – Journal of Death and Dying*, 43, 4, 311–30.

Sharp, P (2000) 'Promoting emotional literacy: emotional literacy improves and increases your life chances', *Pastoral Care*, 18, 3, 8–10.

Sharp, P and Faupel, A (eds) (2002) *Promoting Educational Literacy: Guidelines for Schools, Local Authorities and the Health Services*. Southampton: Emotional Literacy Group, Southampton City Council Local Education Authority.

Sharp, S and Cowie, H (1998) *Counselling and Supporting Children in Distress*. London: Sage.

Shaw, M and others (1999) *The Widening Gap: Health Inequalities and Poverty in Britain*. Bristol: Polity Press.

Shears, J 'Managing tragedy in a secondary school', in Smith, SC and Pennells, M (eds) (1995) *Interventions with Bereaved Children*. London: Jessica Kingsley.

Sheras, PL (2000) *Grief and Traumatic Loss: What Schools Need to Know and Do*. Washington, DC: Hospice Foundation of America.

Shoor, M and Speed, M 'Death, delinquency and the mourning process', in Fulton, R (ed) (1963) *Death and Identity*. Barie, MD: Charles Press.

Shilling, C (1993) *The Body and Social Theory*. London: Sage.

Silverman, P (2000) 'When parents die', in Doka, KJ (ed) (2000) *Living with Grief: Children, Adolescents and Loss*. Washington, DC: Hospice Foundation of America.

Small, N and Hockey, J (2001) *Discourse into Practice: The Production of Bereavement Care*. Buckingham: Open University Press.

Smith, S and Browne, J (2004) 'Feeling Alone ... At the Hospital', paper presented at the Childhood Bereavement Network Conference, *Feeling Alone, Feeling Different*, London.

Sorensen, JR (1989) 'Responding to student or teacher death: preplanning crisis intervention', *Journal of Counseling and Development*, 67, 7, 426–27.

Spall, B and Jordan, G (1999) 'Teachers' perspectives on working with children experiencing loss', *Pastoral Care*, 17, 3, 3–7.

Stevenson, RG (2000) *The Role of Death Education in Helping Children to Cope with Loss*. Washington, DC: Hospice Foundation of America.

Stokes, J, Wyver, S and Crossley, D (1997) 'The challenge of evaluating a bereavement programme', *Palliative Medicine*, 11, 179–90.

Stokes, J and others (1999) 'Developing services for bereaved children: a discussion of the theoretical and practical issues involved', *Mortality*, 4, 3, 291–309.

Strange, J (2002) '"She cried a very little": death, grief and mourning in working-class culture', *Social History*, 27, 2, 143–55.

Stuber, J and others (2002) 'Determinants of counselling for children in Manhattan after the September 11 attacks', *Psychiatric Services*, 53, 7, 815–22.

Sutcliffe, P and others (1998) *Working with the Dying and Bereaved: Systemic Approaches to Therapeutic Work*. London: Macmillan.

Sweeting, H and others (1998) 'Teenage family life, lifestyles and life chances: associations with family structure, conflict with parents, and joint family activity', *International Journal of Law, Policy and the Family*, 12, 1, 15–46.

Tedeschi, RG 'Support groups for bereaved adolescents', in Corr, CA and Balk, DE (eds) (1996) *Handbook of Adolescent Death and Bereavement*. New York: Springer.

Thompson, N (ed) (2002) *Loss and Grief: A Guide for Human Services Practitioners*. Basingstoke: Palgrave.

Tyson-Rawson, KJ 'Adolescent response to the death of a parent', in Corr, CA and Balk, DE (eds) (1996) *Handbook of Adolescent Death and Bereavement*. New York: Springer.

Wadsworth, M (1979) *Roots of Delinquency: Infancy, Adolescence and Crime*. Oxford: Martin Robertson.

Wadsworth, MEJ 'Early stress and associations with adult health, behaviour and parenting', in Butler, NR and Corner, BD (eds) (1984) *Stress and Disability in Childhood*. Bristol: John Wright.

Wadsworth, MEJ (1991) *The Imprint of Time, Childhood, History and Adult Life*. Oxford: Clarendon Press.

Wallbank, S (1991) *Facing Grief: Bereavement and the Young Adult*. Cambridge: Lutterworth Press.

Wallbank, S (1998) *When My Father Died*. London: Cruse Bereavement Care.

Walter, T (1991) 'Modern death: taboo or not taboo?', *Sociology*, 25, 2, 293–310.

Walter, T (1999) *On Bereavement: The Culture of Grief*. Buckingham: Open University Press.

Ward, B (1996) *Good Grief: Exploring Feelings, Loss and Death with under Elevens: A Holistic Approach.* London: Jessica Kingsley.

Webb, NB 'Lay therapy to help bereaved children', in Doka, KJ (ed) (2000) *Living with Grief: Children, Adolescents and Loss.* Washington, DC: Hospice Foundation of America.

Wells, LE and Rankin, JH (1991) 'Families and delinquency: a meta-analysis of the impact of broken homes', *Social Problems*, 38, 1, 71-93.

West, DJ and Farrington, DP (1973) *Who Becomes Delinquent?* London: Heinemann.

Wyn, J and White, R (1997) *Rethinking Youth.* London: Sage.

Wilby, J 'Transcultural counselling: bereavement counselling with adolescents', in Smith, SC and Pennells, M (eds) (1995) *Interventions with Bereaved Children.* London: Jessica Kingsley.

Wilson, A and others (2003) *Schools and Family Change: School Based Support for Children Experiencing Divorce and Separation.* York: Joseph Rowntree Foundation.

Wolfe, BS and Senta, LM (1995) *Intervention with Bereaved Children Nine to Thirteen Years of Age: From a Medical Centre-based Young Person's Grief Support Programme.* New York: Baywood.

Wolfe, BS and Senta, LM 'Interventions with bereaved children nine to thirteen years of age: from a medical center-based young person's grief support program', in Adams, DW and Deveau, EJ (eds) (2002) *Beyond the Innocence of Childhood Vol 3. Helping Children and Adolescents Cope with Death and Bereavement.* New York: Baywood Publishing.

Wood, C and Baulkwill, J 'Sharing experiences – the value of groups for bereaved children', in Smith, SC and Pennells, M (eds) (1995) *Interventions with Bereaved Children.* London: Jessica Kingsley.

Woodhead, M and Montgomery, H (2003) *Understanding Childhood: An Interdisciplinary Approach.* London: John Wiley and Sons.

Worden, JW (1996) *Children and Grief: When a Parent Dies.* New York: Guilford Press.

Worden, JW, Davies, B and McCown, D (1999) 'Comparing parent loss with sibling loss', *Death Studies*, 23, 1, 1–15.

Zall, DS (1994) 'The long-term effects of childhood bereavement – impact on roles as mothers', *Omega – Journal of Death and Dying*, 29, 3, 219–30.